20 GREAT HISTORIC DAY TRIPS

Exploring Long Island

with Newsday

Joan Reminick

A Newsday Book

*To my husband, Burt,
who, in this project
as in all else,
has been there for me
in every way imaginable.*

Copyright 1998 by Newsday Inc.
All Rights Reserved
Published by Newsday, Inc.
235 Pinelawn Road
Melville, N.Y. 11747-4250

No part of this book may be reproduced or transmitted in
any form or by any means, electronic or mechanical,
including photocopying, recording or by any information
storage and retrieval system, without permission in
writing from the publisher.

Printed in Brentwood, N.Y.
ISBN 1885134-13-4

Newsday books are available at special discounts for sales
promotions, premiums, fund-raising or educational use.
For information on bulk purchases, contact:
Marketing Department
Newsday Inc.
235 Pinelawn Road
Melville, N.Y. 11747-4250

ACKNOWLEDGMENTS

For her unflagging encouragement, enthusiasm and keen editorial eye, I wish to thank Newsday Assistant Managing Editor Phyllis Singer. Special thanks, too, to Barbara Marlin, who kept the flow going.

I am also grateful to Newsday Editorial Department members: Vice President for Content Development / Managing Editor Howard Schneider, Executive Editor Bob Keane, Director of Electronic Publishing Peter Bengelsdorf, Executive News Editor Jack Millrod, Editorial Art Director Bob Eisner, Graphics Editor Tim Drachlis, Photography Editor Tony Jerome and Copy Editors Annabelle Kerins and Jeff Pijanowski.

For their cheerful professional assistance, my heartfelt gratitude to those working on Newsday's Long Island History Project who've offered direction and answered my questions, whether small or large: Rhoda Amon, Harvey Aronson, Bill Bleyer, George DeWan, Michelle Ingrassia and Steve Wick. From the Food Department, my thanks to Kari Granville, Carol Bennett and Peter Gianotti.

For allowing me to tap his architectural expertise, I am grateful to Robert McKay, director of the Society for the Preservation of Long Island Antiquities. Thanks, too, to Lynn Seligman for her ongoing guidance and assistance.

I never could have written this book without the active encouragement and in-the-field participation of family and friends. So, in alphabetical order, thanks to Sylvia Carter, Jennie Cuilwik, Kim Darrow, Eleanor Diskin, Roberta Israeloff, Jill and Al Jarnow, A. Reminick, D. Reminick, Judy and Bernie Reminick, Lorraine and Jack Rice, Eileen Runyan, Ken and Sue Schwinn, Doris Weissman.

— *Joan Reminick*

**Illustrated Maps by
Oliver Williams**

Maps are for general location, they do not show all the roads mentioned in the directions. If you are unfamiliar with a specific tour location, we recommend you bring along a detailed road map.

TABLE OF CONTENTS

Foreword VI

Acknowledgments VIII

The Tours

The Gold Coast /I 1
Westbury House and Old Westbury Gardens
Sands Point Preserve: Falaise

The Gold Coast /II 7
Eagle's Nest/Vanderbilt Museum
Coe Hall

Historic Oyster Bay 14
Sagamore Hill
Raynham Hall
Oyster Bay Historic Society/Earle-Wightman House

East Hampton's Treasures 22
Home Sweet Home, Pollock-Krasner House
Clinton Academy, Mulford Farm

Amagansett and Montauk......... 30
Marine Museum / Amagansett
Miss Amelia Cottage / Amagansett
Roy K. Lester Carriage Museum
Second House
Third House
Montauk Lighthouse

Sag Harbor: The Whaling Life 39
The Custom House
Sag Harbor Whaling and Historical Museum
Sag Harbor Fire Department Museum

The North Fork 46
Historic Museums of Southold
Horton's Point Lighthouse
Oysterponds Historical Society

Major Thomas Jones' Island 53
Old Grace Church Complex
Jones Beach: Castles in the Sand

Paumanok: A Writer's Island 60
Cedarmere
The Knothole
Walt Whitman's Birthplace

South Shore Sampler............ 67
Wantagh Preservation Society and Museum
Seaford Historical Society
Amityville Historical Society/Lauder Museum

When Queens Was Young......... 74
King Manor / Jamaica
Grace Church / Jamaica
Queens County Farm / Floral Park

Huntington Heritage............. 81
David Conklin Farmhouse
Dr. Daniel Kissam House
Suydam Homestead and Barn Museum

Hempstead and Garden City....... 88
St. George's Episcopal Church
African American Museum
Cathedral of the Incarnation

North Shore Nassau 95
Garvie's Point
Sands / Willet House
Merchant Marine Museum

The Stony Brook Route.......... 103
Thompson House
Museums at Stony Brook, Caleb Smith House
Deepwells, St. James General Store
St. James Episcopal Church

Old Riverhead 113
Railroad Museum of Long Island
Hallockville Museum Farm and Folklife Center
Suffolk County Historical Society

Cold Spring Harbor / Lloyd Neck .. 120
Joseph Lloyd House
Cold Spring Harbor Whaling Museum
Cold Spring Harbor Fish Hatchery

The South Shore Gold Coast...... 129
West Sayville Marine Museum
Meadow Croft
Bayard Cutting Arboretum
Connetquot River State Park Preserve

Old Bethpage Village Restoration.. 137

The Drive-By Architectural Tours . 143

One-Stop Destinations........... 152

The Wineries of Long Island...... 159

FOREWORD

You are an adventurous person — a searcher, an inquirer who looks beyond the obvious to seek out the hidden. This I know because you — or else someone who knows you well — bought this book. And it is, after all, a book about exploring.

Until recently, I knew relatively little about what Long Island had to offer in historical attractions. Restaurants, I could tell you about. Shopping? Don't get me started. But if you'd asked me about the history of my own neighborhood, you'd have gotten little more than a noncommittal shrug.

And then Newsday began its history project, Long Island: Our Story. The more I read, the more I began to understand the scope, depth and quality of what Long Island was all about. Still, it was one thing to encounter historical figures on a page; to know them in the intimacy of their own surroundings was quite another.

Hence, this book. For me, the research was one revelation after another. I read of love affairs, spy rings, murders and hauntings. I learned about shipwrecks and about those who risked their lives to save crew and passengers. I visited the studio of a great artist who lived too hard and died too young, spent time at the birthplace of a genius poet who sacrificed his health to tend to wounded soldiers, encountered the work of a brilliant Long Island architect whose infidelities led to a murder that shocked the world.

What shocked me most was how often I ended up surprised by what I encountered. Had I imagined that the American Merchant Marine Museum — housed in a magnificent mansion — would be the emotionally moving, eye-opening experience it was? Could I have anticipated that a visit to Garvies Point Museum would evoke nostalgic memories of childhood trips to the Museum of Natural History in Manhattan? Or that from a visit to the Seaford Historical Society — a cavernous room filled with rusty tools, antique furniture and old photographs — I'd come away feeling well-acquainted with some of the people who'd helped shape the destiny of a town? Those antiquities and artifacts would probably have been meaningless without the sparkling anecdotes provided by the person in charge of that collection.

Which brings me to what has been most rewarding aspect of my explorations: the people. It is the impassioned, dedicated and lively individuals working to preserve, restore and present these exhibits who, in the end, make them true attractions. I'll never forget one woman in her 70s, a volunteer who energetically led me on an outdoor tour on a sultry summer day when I was ready to wilt. Or the very serious director of a major museum who, in hushed tones, took me aside to tell me about a nearby attraction that he strongly believed was haunted. "I've got photographic proof," he said.

I picked up lots of trivia along the way. Did you know that that Long Islanders whose families have been here for over a century pronounce the name "Montauk" with the stress on the second syllable — "monTAUK," while arrivistes such as myself emphasize the first syllable, "MONtauk." And then, of course, there's the tidbit I first heard at the Earle-Wightman House in Oyster Bay and then, it seemed, at every other old house I visited: early rope beds had to be constantly tightened with a key; hence the origins of the phrase "sleep tight."

Of course, we couldn't include every attraction on Long Island in this one volume; some omissions were unavoidable. You won't, for example, find Rock Hall in Lawrence because during the writing of this book, that pre-Revolutionary home was under restoration and inaccessible. Other sites, too, had to be excluded, some because they weren't open for an off-season viewing, others because of limited space in this book. And the projected Cradle of Aviation Museum at Mitchel Field is still under construction, its opening date at least a year away.

What you will find are twenty trips, all do-able within a day. Taken together, they offer a representative picture of what's out there. For the sake of both convenience and variety, most itineraries were planned according to geography rather than theme. There's also a list of one-stop destinations and a guide to Long Island's burgeoning wine country.

Feel free to mix and match. And if you're suddenly overcome by the sensation that you've looked at too many sites in one day, by all means, stop. Go shopping. Go out to eat — this book is filled with restaurant tips.

And have fun. Because there's a wealth of living history waiting for you. The more you see, the deeper your understanding will be of what you already know: that Long Island, next-door-neighbor to the Big Apple, is, in its own right, a real plum.

— *Joan Reminick*

THE GOLD COAST / I

During the enchanted era between the Gilded Age and the Roaring '20s, a mythic kingdom of millionaires grew up on Long Island's North Shore. They built palaces, sailed yachts, threw parties, played polo, owned fast horses and drove faster cars.

Yet Long Island's Gold Coast was more than just a millionaire's playground. It was also a seat of great philanthropy and a spawning ground for scientific, artistic and technological achievement.

Thanks to the engaging, well-informed volunteers who conduct tours of these mansions, we get to hear the inside stories of their original owners.

Westbury House And Old Westbury Gardens

In 1903, when John (Jay) Phipps of the Carnegie Steel Co. millions tied the knot with British-born Margarita Grace of the Grace Shipping Lines, it was with the promise to build her a proper English estate. With the help of London architect George Crawley, Phipps oversaw the construction of a Charles II manor house, a reasonable facsimile of Battle Abbey, Margarita's childhood home. It took from 1904 to 1907 to complete Westbury House and Old Westbury Gardens, but oh, what a wedding present!

You'll approach via the Linden Allee, a towering corridor of trees that eventually leads to the parking lot booth where you'll pay a $10 admission fee to both the house and the gardens. To do them justice, start at 10 a.m., when the property opens, and allow at least half a day. Expect, also, to walk a lot and in summer, see the gardens first because it gets hot in the afternoon.

Your garden and house tour lead you through intricately landscaped formal gardens, evoking images

Newsday Photo / Bill Davis
The Phipps Mansion at Old Westbury Gardens

of the past. You'll see a pond with a replica of the Phipps children's sailboat and, near the fragrant Lilac Walk, a little cemetery where much-loved family pets are buried and the miniature Thatched Cottage set up for a doll's tea party.

This was the Phipps' 10th birthday gift to their daughter Peggie, who is now in her 90s and lives elsewhere on the property. Perhaps Peggie was the favorite, it has been suggested; note too the three modest log cabins belonging to the Phipps boys.

Within the beautiful Walled Garden, you'll find all kinds of trees and shrubbery that have been trained to grow on walls. In the Lower Garden, rows of white flowers are arranged in the motif of the double strand of pearls favored by Mrs. Phipps. Another highlight is the hemlock-planted Ghost Allee, a replica of the yew walk at Battle Abbey.

Then there's the manor itself, both awe-inspiring and surprisingly homey. The front hall, with its dark wood pillars and archways, showcases the gorgeous chimney piece of sculptor Frances Derwent Wood as well as the ceiling of English Decorative painter, A. Duncan Carse. Be sure to find out why the house has only one closet. And check out Mrs. Phipps' library, a small gem rich in the details of family life.

Perhaps the best room is the West Porch, whose glass walls are made to retract into the basement on hydraulic lifts. Imagine sitting under a magnificent coffered oak ceiling surrounded only by Ionic columns and the summer breeze. Reclining on an oversized chintz couch, you wait while tea is brought up on a dumb-waiter whose outline is still visible in the marble floor.

Other must-sees: the surprisingly modern White Drawing Room, with a self-portrait of son Michael Phipps, the formal Red Ballroom whose French doors open onto a scenic terrace, and Mr. Phipps' Green Study filled with family pictures, trophies and a solid silver chandelier.

The dining room is especially impressive when one takes into account that Jay Phipps had it brought — walls and all — from the Fifth Avenue townhouse of his father, Henry Phipps, and reassembled here in 1927. And the art: a Gainsborough hangs on one wall, while another holds a John Singer Sargent portrait of Jay Phipps' sister Amy holding her baby grandson, Winston Guest. Can you guess who the baby's godfather was? (Clue: Winston.)

Upstairs, check out the lovely armoires and explore the bedrooms where, via portraits and photographs, you'll find a fascinating picture of family life emerging.

It should be somewhere about noon when you've finished.

You'll want want to stop for lunch before heading northwest to the Sands Point Preserve to view Falaise.

Sands Point Preserve: Falaise

Castlegould is the medieval-looking structure you'll come upon when you drive into the Sands Point Preserve in Port Washington. A knockoff of Kilkenny Castle in Ireland, it originally served as stables and servants quarters for Howard Gould, whose father, railroad magnate Jay Gould, bought the property in 1900. Today, it houses a range of changing exhibits and serves as a welcome center.

Nearby is the imposing Tudor manor called Hempstead House that Gould built for his Irish bride, but the couple divorced before work was completed. In 1917, Gould sold it to Daniel Guggenheim, whose family fortune had been made in mining. Although there is much to see at Hempstead House, including the formidable Buten Wedgwood collection, the main attraction on Sands Point is Falaise, the Normandy style manor Guggenheim's son Harry built in 1923 on the 90 acres his father had given him as a wedding present.

The name, which is French for "cliff," aptly describes the house perched high over Long Island Sound. Once a nearly self-sufficient feudal estate with farm animals and orchards, Falaise was constructed using architectural bits and pieces from medieval and Renaissance estates and castles from Europe.

It is a house whose owner, Harry Guggenheim, made history. Guggenheim, a publisher, a U.S. Navy captain, and a race-horse owner, also was an intimate friend of pioneer aviator Charles Lindbergh. At Falaise, Guggenheim's second wife, Carol Potter Morton, introduced Lindbergh to aeronautical

Directions

To Old Westbury Gardens (Phipps Estate)
Long Island Expressway to exit 39 south (Glen Cove Road). From west, stay on service road; if coming from east, make left onto service road. At first light, turn right to Old Westbury Road. Entrance is a quarter-mile on left.

To Sands Point Preserve (Falaise: Guggenheim Estate)
Long Island Expressway to exit 36 (Searingtown Road). Go north six miles straight to entrance on right. From Old Westbury Gardens, take a right at gate onto Old Westbury Road to Long Island Expressway westbound service road; right at Guinea Woods Road; left at Northern Boulevard (Route 25A); right at Middle Neck Road — go north about five miles to entrance.

---

scientist Robert Goddard. The Guggenheims suggested that Lindbergh oversee Goddard and five colleagues in a rocketry project they were working on in the desert of New Mexico.

For 23 years, Harry Guggenheim supported that operation, which eventually evolved into the U.S. space program.

In the carport you'll see Lindbergh's old station wagon, which he drove to the house the day the Nassau County Department of Parks opened it to the public in 1973. Our guide offered some recollections of the house tour she'd given Charles and Anne Morrow Lindbergh that day.

If you're lucky, you might get to hear fascinating Lindbergh anecdotes on your tour.

After Guggenheim married his third wife, Alicia Patterson, he purchased a defunct newspaper in Hempstead, marking the birth of Newsday with

Harry as publisher and Alicia as editor.

Significantly, in one of the upstairs corridors, there is a plaque with a 1969 Newsday front page that reads "Man Walks on the Moon." It is signed by Bill Moyers, publisher at that time, as well as members of the staff, and reads: "Congratulations to Captain Guggenheim who has made many dreams come true."

Aside from the awe-inspiring art collection that ranges from a Giacometti sculpture to a Della Robia plate, there are the incomparable views of the water. Gaze out over the Sound from the breakfast porch and imagine Alicia and Harry discussing their newspaper business. These were not the idle rich.

Important Information

Old Westbury Gardens (Phipps Estate)
71 Old Westbury Rd.
Old Westbury
516-333-0048

Open: Late April to mid-December, Wednesday to Monday (closed Tuesdays) 10 a.m. to 5 p.m.
Fee: Adults, $10; seniors, $7; children 6-12, $6.
Tours: Yes
Rest rooms: Three. In house, near walled garden, near plant shed
On-site food: Outdoor cafe
Wheelchair access: Yes
Gift shop: In main house
Child appropriate: For older children

Sands Point Preserve, Falaise: Guggenheim Estate
95 Middle Neck Rd.
Sands Point
516-571-7900

Open: May to October, Wednesday to Sunday, noon to 3 p.m.
Fee: Adults $5; seniors, $4
Tours: Yes
Rest rooms: Only at Castlegould
On-site food: Snack bar at Castlegould
Wheelchair access: Not to Falaise or Hempstead House; only Castlegould
Gift shop: At Castlegould
Child appropriate: For older children

Where to Eat

Cafe In the Woods
Old Westbury Gardens
516-334-9557
If you're really pressed for time, you could remain at Old Westbury Gardens and grab a sandwich or salad at Cafe In the Woods, where the food is basic and reasonably priced.

DeSeversky Conference Center
On Northern Boulevard
Old Westbury
516-626-1600
In keeping with the Gold Coast mansion motif, you could stop at this center, formerly the Alfred I. Dupont estate White Eagle, which later became Templeton when it belonged to Amy Phipps Guest, sister of John Phipps. There, a buffet lunch, made by culinary students at the New York Institute of Technology, costs about $15, and the surroundings are quite something.

Montgomery's Restaurant & Bar
235 Roslyn Rd.
Roslyn Heights
516-625-5553
Here the walls are hung with old Gold Coast photographs. The well-executed contemporary American fare is moderately priced.

The Roslyn Bread Company
400 Willis Ave.
Roslyn Heights
516-625-1470
This is a fine choice for a sandwich on one of their marvelous homemade breads. Salads and pastas rate highly, too.

Salvatore's Coal Oven Pizzeria
124 Shore Rd.
Port Washington
516-883-8457
Closer to the Sands Point Preserve, you could get a fine individual pizza here and be out in less than half an hour for well under $10 a person. Millionaires understand the value of thrift.

THE GOLD COAST/II

Ask most people where Long Island's Gold Coast ends and they'll probably tell you the Nassau-Suffolk county line. Actually, the Gold Coast extends through Huntington all the way to Centerport, where William Kissam Vanderbilt built his summer estate, Eagle's Nest.

On this tour, you'll visit that home, part of the Vanderbilt Museum, as well as Coe Hall, part of the Planting Fields Arboretum complex in Oyster Bay. Because the Vanderbilt estate opens at noon — earlier than Coe Hall by half an hour — that's where you'll probably want to start.

Wherever you opt to begin, though, time is tight, so take care not to spend too much time between sites.

Eagle's Nest
Vanderbilt Museum

Did you know that the term "conspicuous consumption" was first coined in reference to the spending habits of the Vanderbilt family? This is just one of many informative tidbits you'll pick up while touring Vanderbilt's Moorish-looking mansion.

But William Kissam Vanderbilt, the Vanderbilt affectionately known as Willie K., did much more than just conspicuously spend his family's vast fortune. He was a millionaire with vision. Case in point: An avid racing-car driver, Vanderbilt became frustrated with the dusty condition of the roads. Rather than gripe, he had the Long Island Motor Parkway built. Running from Queens to Suffolk, it became the world's first concrete-paved motorway. (Part of the parkway, now called the Vanderbilt Motor Parkway, still runs from Dix

The master bedroom of the Vanderbilt Museum

Newsday Photo / J. Michael Dombroski

Hills to Lake Ronkonkoma.)

Vanderbilt, was a public-spirited man. At his death in 1920, he bequeathed to Suffolk County his home and all its surrounding property, including a museum that, in its day, was considered among the nation's most impressive.

Vanderbilt purchased Eagle's Nest in 1906, but it wasn't until his later years that he expanded the house and gave it a Spanish look. You'll start your tour in the stately library, off a Morroccan-tiled courtyard. Among the family portraits is one of Willie K.'s sister, Consuelo, who was unhappily married to the Duke of Marlborough; another depicts Vanderbilt's mother, Alva, who, in addition to being a pivotal figure on the New York social scene, was an ardent feminist who helped Susan B. Anthony pass the 19th Amendment.

The history of the Vanderbilt wealth dates to 1794 and the birth of Willie K.'s grandfather Cornelius (Commodore) Vanderbilt on Staten Island. Poor but resourceful, Cornelius started a boat service that became the first Staten Island Ferry. He invested well, buying, first, steamboats and then railroads. During the California Gold Rush, he ferried people from New York to California. At age 83, Cornelius died with more money than the U.S. Treasury.

It was a Vanderbilt who made Madison Square Garden a sports arena, who opened the Metropolitan Museum of Art, and who founded the Metropolitan Opera. Willie K., descended from such stock, grew up during the Gilded Age in the fashion of European royalty.

Reflecting this royal bent, Vanderbilt filled his home with examples of superb craftsmanship and artistry culled from all over the world. He collected church treasures and religious art. He hobnobbed with celebrities, and the guest bedrooms were frequented by many an illustrious name. Sonja Henie slept in the yellow room, while the Duke and Duchess of Windsor, guests at many a millionaire's mansion, took up residence down the hall. There must have been many a lively evening spent in the music room, which had been specially built to house Vanderbilt's 1918 Aolian pipe organ.

The master bedroom is filled with Napoleonic artifacts — most notably, a reproduction of Bonaparte's campaign bed. There are pictures of Willie K. as a boy, photos of his mother, for whom his last yacht was named, and a painting over the bed of the yacht. Reputed to be the most powerful and luxurious yacht in the world, the Alva was equipped with seaplanes and its own movie theater. It also was the first private yacht to fly the naval reserve flag, but in 1943 was sunk by a German U-boat.

Willie K.'s first marriage was to Virginia Graham Fair in 1899, and it was an unhappy union. Still, it produced three children. In 1927 Vanderbilt married Rosamund Lancaster, with whom he'd fallen in love when she was still married to her first husband, a photographer named Richard Warburton. The Warburtons had accompanied Vanderbilt on a South Pacific cruise, and the rest is history.

A study in luxury, Rosamund's boudoir features a circular dressing room with an entire wall serving as a mirror. Check out the bathroom with its solid marble tub and regal commode.

Then, there is the memorial wing, with a room devoted to Willie K.'s son, who was killed in an auto accident while on safari. You'll also see a scale model of the Alva as well as trophies and photographs of Willie's racing and yachting days. Other exhibits showcase bird life and invertebrates.

You have to go outside and walk around to the Habitat Wing, an unusual museumlike adjunct to the house, which houses life-sized tableaux of scenes from Vanderbilt's travels. If you detect a resemblance to the dioramas in the the Museum of Natural History in New York, it's because the same taxidermy and style of art work was used.

It's a short walk from the house to the museum itself, which opened in 1922 and includes the Hall of Fishes. There, you'll see a number of marine specimens, some real, others plaster of paris. William Belanske, known as the Audubon of the fish world, did many of the renderings depicting the specimens on display, some of which are preserved, a bit grotesquely, in alcohol and water.

Coe Hall

At the dawn of the 20th Century, anything seemed possible in America. That was when William R. Coe, a young English immigrant, rose

Directions

To Vanderbilt Museum
Long Island Expressway to exit 49 north (Route 110). Go north about eight miles into Huntington village. Turn right on Route 25A (Main Street). Go east about 3½ miles to Little Neck Road. Turn left on Little Neck Road and proceed a mile to museum. If coming from Coe Hall, take Route 25A west through Huntington village. Follow directions above.

To Coe Hall
Long Island Expressway to exit 41 north. Go to Route 106, following it into Oyster Bay. Turn left onto Lexington Avenue. At next light, Mill River Road, turn left. After a quarter of a mile, follow sign to Planting Fields Arboretum. If coming from Vanderbilt Museum, take Route 25A west to Route 106. Follow the directions above from Lexington Avenue.

---

from the job of office boy at an insurance company to chairman of the board. It didn't hurt Coe's ascent that he married Mai Rogers, daughter of H.H. Rogers, a founder of the Standard Oil Co.

The couple leased the estate known as Planting Fields (from the Matinecock Indian name) and in 1913, bought it. But the Queen Anne house on the property had burned to the ground so Coe hired the New York firm of Walker & Gilette to design the new Coe Hall. Over the next three years, a 65-room Tudor Revival house faced in Indiana limestone rose on the old foundations. Characterized by beautiful carved stone and wood, timbered windows, and

Newsday Photo / J. Michael Dombroski

The lush gardens around the reflecting pool at Coe Hall

stained glass, its design closely paralleled that of St. Catherine's Court, a former convent in Bath, England, that currently is a bed and breakfast owned by actress Jane Seymour.

You'll enter through a Tudor archway whose carvings speak of Coe's background in maritime insurance as well as his love of the hunt. The den, with its exquisite wood paneling and 16th-Century soapstone fireplace, features a firescreen with intricate wrought iron designs by Samuel Yellin, a Polish artist who was also a favorite with the Vanderbilts. Look up at the beautiful strapwork ceiling, which resembles an overhead chenille bedspread.

Although, you may not be able to take the main staircase upstairs to the 11 bedrooms and 11 baths, because of renovations, you can admire the graceful bannisters, more of Samuel Yellin's artistry. Be sure to check out the telephone room, a cozy little nook with a special appeal for teens.

Particularly engaging are photographs of the 1934 wedding of Coe's strikingly beautiful daughter, Natalie, to the Italian Count Vitetti — a special dispensation from the Pope was granted to hold the ceremony at home. The couple took their vows in the Great Hall, at a marble altar modeled after the one at St. Patrick's cathedral; some of the stained glass windows came from Anne Boleyn's home in England. The groom, incidentally, happened to be a fascist, and Natalie spent much of World War II in hiding.

Coe himself had a love affair with the American West. This is apparent in the paintings and sculptures as well as the Buffalo Bill memorabilia on display. But nowhere is Coe's ardor more manifest than in the extraordinary breakfast room, whose four walls are covered with a three-dimensional Western mural done in gesso by the artist Robert Chandler, who depicts buffalo and elk roaming a great plain.

Coe spent little time at Planting Fields after his wife died, at age 49. Two years later, he married Carolyn Slaughter, who preferred the hunting lodge Coe bought for her in South Carolina. Carolyn is remembered for the stinging comment she made regarding the Duke and Duchess of Windsor, professional houseguests extraordinaire: "They stay too long."

Once outside, stroll past the reflecting pond to the Tea House, which is perhaps the most remarkable sight of all. Designed by artist Everett Shinn, the miniature country French cottage was built as a play house for Natalie. Adults as well as children will be enchanted by the interior — the pastel murals, as well as the birds and flower baskets that grace the hand-painted andirons, all done by Shinn. As you depart, be sure to visit the aptly named Camellia House filled with blooms and charming statuary.

Important Information

Vanderbilt Museum
180 Little Neck Rd.
  Centerport
  516-854-5555

Open: Year-round Tuesday to Sunday, noon to 4 p.m.
Fee: $5; $3 over 60 and students, $1 children; additional $3 for mansion tour
Tours: No
Rest rooms: In all buildings
On-site food: No
Wheelchair access: Not at mansion
Gift shop: Yes, in Planetarium
Child appropriate: For older children

Coe Hall
  Planting Fields Road
  Oyster Bay
516-922-9210

Open: April to September daily, noon to 3:30 p.m.
Fee: $5 adults, $3.50 seniors; $1 children 7-12, under 6 free
Tours: Of Arboretum available for groups only
Rest rooms: Yes, in front of main greenhouse
On-site food: No, just soda machines
Wheelchair access: Yes, on main floor of house
Gift shop: Yes, in Coe Hall
Child appropriate: For older children

Where to Eat

Near Vanderbilt Museum

Petite on Main
328 Main St.
Huntington
516-271-3311
This spot offers light, creative fare in friendly environs.

Munday's
259 Main St.
Huntington
516-421-3553
At this vintage luncheonette the surroundings are a bit dark, but char-grilled burgers are tops; they serve breakfast, too.

Tortilla Grill
335 New York Ave.
Huntington
516-423-4141
If you're looking for a quick fix, Tex-Mex style, this spot may have just the taco for you.

Trio's
67 Wall St.
Huntington
516-673-8888
Try it for salads, pastas, sandwiches, or just capuccino and dessert.

Near Coe Hall

Canterbury Ales Oyster Bar & Grill
46 Audrey Ave.
Oyster Bay
516-922-3614
They open for lunch at 11:30 a.m. The food is hearty, interesting, and moderately priced.

The Country Inn
19 Oyster Bay Rd.
Locust Valley
516-676-9670
Although it opens at noon, it is literally down the street from Coe Hall. Salads are fresh and flavorsome.

HISTORIC OYSTER BAY

The spirit of Theodore Roosevelt hovers benignly over Oyster Bay, a quaint seaside town that has nurtured its share of American characters, from a turn-of-the-century president to a Revolutionary War spy-hero, from some of the nation's wealthiest industrialists to simple tradesfolk, farmers and fishermen.

Sagamore Hill

"There could be no healthier and pleasanter place in which to bring up children than in that nook of old-time America around Sagamore Hill," wrote Teddy Roosevelt, whose beloved homestead remains the area's foremost attraction. It's a good idea to sign up as early as possible for a tour, since groups fill quickly, especially on summer weekends. If the morning tours are sold out, buy afternoon tickets and visit the other sites first.

Before or after you see the main house, stroll across the parking lot to the Old Orchard Museum, former home to Roosevelt's son Theodore Jr., to see a short but moving video biography of Theodore Roosevelt. Afterwards, amble through rooms filled with old family photographs and artifacts.

Back at the main house, you can wait for your tour sitting in one of the original rocking chairs on the porch of this extraordinary and yet typically American home, inhabited by the Roosevelt family from 1887 to 1948. Decorated the way it was during the presidential years, 1901-1909, Sagamore Hill centered around the six Roosevelt children: Alice, whose mother, Alice Lee, died in childbirth in 1884, before the house was completed, and the offspring of T.R.'s marriage two years later to Edith Kermit Carow — Theodore Jr., Kermit, Ethel, Archie and Quentin. There were pets, too: a mountain lion, a brown bear and a badger named Josiah to name a few. By the way, the stuffed badger you'll see on tour is not Josiah; he went to the Bronx Zoo.

Sagamore Hill National Historic Site / National Parks Service
A view into the dining room at Sagamore Hill

The profusion of animal pelts and parts that decorate the house were the result of Roosevelt's exploits while on African safari for the Smithsonian. In the hall, you'll see the head of the cape buffalo that charged Roosevelt and his son Kermit, stopped by a timely well-placed bullet. See if you can find the elephant's-foot wastepaper basket and rhino-foot bookends elsewhere in the house. The dark, book-lined library, with more than 6,000 volumes, is testimony to Roosevelt's voracious two-books-a-day reading appetite. Whatever T.R. was doing, though, he'd stop promptly at 4 p.m. in order to play with his children. Incidentally, ask about the story behind the letter "E" carved into the library wall.

The parlor, painted a delicate blue and set for tea, is home to a stuffed polar bear, given to Edith by Admiral Perry. In the stately maroon-hued dining room, the table is laid out with the original White House china. The imposing North Room, added in 1905, showcases gifts given Roosevelt by both Japan and Russia honoring his negotiation of peace between those two warring nations, for which he won the Nobel Peace prize. There also is a huge German book of the Ring Cycle, a gift of Kaiser Wilhelm. A portrait of Roosevelt in his Rough Rider uniform hangs on the wall, and there are replicas of the flags the regiment carried up San Juan Hill in Cuba during the Spanish-American War of 1898.

After visiting the kitchen (find out what's in the safe), you'll head upstairs. Take note of the "door locked" sign between Alice's room and the boys' quarters, as well as the oversized bathtub where the kids would put snakes and salamanders. In the nursery, you'll see a marvelous Thomas Nast illustration of Santa Claus. Roosevelt's coat, cape and boots look ready for action in the dressing room. The master bedroom is yellow and airy, with a huge carved bed. Next door is daughter Ethel's room, furnished to reflect the period, about 1917, when Ethel Roosevelt Derby moved back to her family home with her two young children while her husband was away at war. The baby paraphernalia — especially the walker — looks surprisingly modern. It's also in that room where, in 1919, Roosevelt died at age 60, sleeping there because of the bed's proximity to the fireplace.

On the top floor is Roosevelt's gun room, where he did much of his voluminous writing. Then, there's Theodore Jr.'s room, with its Long Island Rail Road trains, box camera, Harvard pennant and sports equipment. You'll also see the servants' rooms and the nanny's quarters.

Pause, on the way down, at the family portrait gallery near the guest rooms. Sadly, three of Roosevelt's four sons died in the two world wars — the youngest, Quentin, for whom Roosevelt Field was named, died first. There is a particularly touching picture of Quentin, age 5, in front of the White House, poised with a toy arrow. He ultimately *did* shoot the artist with it, we are told.

Raynham Hall

Is Raynham Hall Museum, the scene of Revolutionary War spy intrigue and thwarted romance, actually haunted? Perhaps.

It started out as a salt-box colonial in 1738 and was purchased shortly thereafter by Quaker merchant and town judge Samuel Townsend. As a Quaker, Townsend did not actively participate in the Revolution, but his sympathies were with the Colonists. When the British occupied his home, Col. John Graves Simcoe, head of the Queen's Rangers, became the uninvited guest-of-honor. Simcoe also became the sweetheart of Townsend's daughter, Sally. What neither Townsend nor Simcoe knew, though, was that Sally's brother Robert, who lived and worked in Manhattan, was a spy for Gen. George

Directions

To Sagamore Hill National Historic Site
Long Island Expressway to exit 41 north (Route 106). Go north on Route 106 toward Oyster Bay and follow signs to Sagamore Hill.

To Raynham Hall Museum
From Sagamore Hill: Left turn at end of Sagamore Hill Road onto Cove Neck Road; at end, turn right onto Oyster Bay Cove Road, which becomes East Main Street. At Route 106 (South Street), make a left and then the next right onto West Main Street; the house will be on your right.

To Oyster Bay Historical Society/ Earle-Wightman House
From Raynham Hall: Continue west on West Main Street half a block, making the first left onto Spring Street and the first left onto Orchard Street. Cross Route 106; Orchard Street becomes Summit Street. Earle-Wightman House will be on your right.

Washington.

One evening, when home alone, Sally discovered and read a message left in a cupboard for Simcoe: Benedict Arnold was about to turn West Point over to the British. Faced with a difficult decision, Sally chose the Colonists over her lover, getting the message to her brother in time to foil Arnold's plot. While Arnold escaped, Maj. John Andre, his co-conspirator, was captured and executed as a spy.

Thereafter, Simcoe broke off all relations with the Townsend family. Sally never married and lived well into her 80s. It is said that her spirit, doomed in love, is still within the walls of the house.

The house remained unchanged until 1851, when Townsend's grandson Solomon built a larger, grander Victorian addition and re-named the place Raynham Hall, after the family's ancestral home in England. It remained in the Townsend family until 1940, when it was given to the Daughters of the American Revolution, who operated it as a museum and tea shop until 1947, when it was turned over to the Town of Oyster Bay. The tea enterprise was discontinued and the house restored to its Colonial appearance, which meant removing many of Solomon's additions.

Today, Raynham Hall is two houses in one. On the first floor of the Colonial section, you'll find an 18th-Century hall, a parlor, trimmed in its original bright turquoise and, in the rear, a spare chamber where Simcoe probably slept. The upstairs Colonial part, accessible through the Victorian addition, houses Samuel's master bedroom as well as the room where Sally and her sisters dwelled.

In contrast is the richly carpeted and wallpapered Victorian section. There's a beautiful music room with an 1839 spinet, a dining room with an unusual pleated ceiling and, in the hallway, an intricately carved coat rack. On the second floor, note the exquisite turn-of-the-century doll house before moving on to an exhibit of photographs of the house in its earlier years. A photo of Solomon Townsend's children in a pony cart circa 1864 is fascinating. You'll also see the beautiful canary-yellow master suite of Solomon Townsend II, with its charming adjoining nursery.

Still, the most intriguing presence in the house remains Sally's.

Oyster Bay Historical Society
Earle-Wightman House

It might look like just another modest white clapboard house, but the Earle-Wightman House, home to the Oyster Bay Historical Society, holds centuries worth of history.

The house was built in 1720 as a one-room dwelling. Gloomy and utilitarian, it's set up to represent the home of a tailor, who, indeed, might have been its first tenant. There's a flax wheel, a

Newsday Photo

The Earle-Wightman House, which was built in 1720

wool wheel and a nail-studded tool called a hackel, all used to fashion cloth out of the flax plant. (Working demonstrations are given regularly by the Historical Society). Near the window is a tailor's bench and accoutrements of the trade. In a corner, you'll find a trundle bed with a rope frame (it's from tightening the frame with a bed key that the expression, "sleep tight" originated).

A lean-to kitchen was added to the house in 1740, and within 30 years, a two-room deep, story-and-a-half addition was put on by the owner, a merchant named William Butler. In 1830, Marmaduke Earle, a Baptist minister renowned for his eloquent marriage ceremonies, added the central hall and stairway, today painted the original yellow and brown colors. In the 1880s, another Baptist minister, Charles S. Wightman married one of Earle's granddaughters and lived in the house until his death in 1934. The somewhat awkward-looking portraits of Mr. and Mrs. George Coles of Glen Cove that hang on the wall were probably done by an itinerant artist who used stock torsos and then painted in the heads.

Further back in the house is an educational room for changing exhibits. The Historical Society works closely with schools, allowing children to try on Revolutionary War uniform reproductions. Continue to the rear door, where you'll find a charming outdoor ornamental garden with a well-head from a nearby farm.

Back inside, near the research library, is an 1833 map of Oyster Bay. Within the library, on a 1900 map, you'll see how the growing town included the Long Island Rail Road, completed in 1889 to transport workers to Gold Coast estates. The library contains a wealth of historic documents and images as well as maps, atlases, genealogies and old town records from 1653-1878. It also includes an impressive Theodore Roosevelt collection. Upstairs, the rooms await restoration and refurbishment, but be sure to see the area behind the cupboard where the original roof line of the house is exposed. It's a window into another century.

Important Information

Sagamore Hill National Historic Site
Sagamore Hill Road
Oyster Bay
516-922-4447

Open: Closed Monday and Tuesday from late October to late April. Otherwise, open daily, 9:30 a.m. to 4 p.m.; the last tour leaves at 4 p.m.
Fee: $5 adults; 16 and under, free
Tours: Yes. Nobody admitted to house unless on tour
Rest rooms: In Visitors Center and Old Orchard Museum
On-site food: No
Wheelchair access: Ramp to first floor only of Sagamore Hill; Old Orchard Museum accessible
Gift shop: In Visitors Center
Child appropriate: Yes

Raynham Hall Museum
20 W. Main St.
Oyster Bay
516-922-6808

Open: Tuesday to Sunday (open Monday only on national holidays), 1 p.m. to 5 p.m.; July 4th to Labor Day, noon to 5 p.m.
Fee: Adults, $3; Children 7 to 21, students with ID cards, and seniors, $2; children under 7 are free
Tours: Self-guided, plus special school tours
Rest rooms: On ground floor
On-site food: No
Wheelchair access: First floor only
Gift Shop: No
Child appropriate: Children over 6

Oyster Bay Historical Society
Earle-Wightman House
20 Summit St.
Oyster Bay
516-922-5032

Open: Research library and museum, Tuesday to Friday, 10 a.m. to 2 p.m., Saturday;, 9 a.m. to 1 p.m.; Sunday 1 p.m. to 4 p.m., or by appointment
Fee: Donation

Tours: Yes
Rest rooms: On ground floor
On-site food: No
Wheelchair access: To first floor of museum but not rest room
Gift shop: Yes, a small one
Child appropriate: Yes

Where to Eat

The Bookmark Cafe
1 E. Main St.
Oyster Bay
516-922-0036
The cafe is a very civilized restaurant-within-a-bookshop, situated in a building Roosevelt's staff used as a reception office for visitors to Sagamore Hill. The menu is creative and well-executed, especially at lunch time, when such items as grilled salmon, lettuce and tomato with herb mayonnaise or chicken and mozzarella quesadilla with cilantro and avocado puree may be the order of the day.

Cafe Al Dente
2 Spring St.
Oyster Bay
516-922-2442
This is a homey little trattoria where the fine, chewy-crusted pizzas vie with an array of vibrant pasta dishes. In warmer weather, there's also outdoor seating.

Calamari Kitchen
62B South St.
Oyster Bay
516-922-2999
Calamari Kitchen has an open kitchen that turns out some inspired Italian seafood, featuring squid in a variety of unconventional preparations.

EAST HAMPTON'S TREASURES

Did you know that East Hampton was once known as Maidstone? Or that Main Street, now lined with trendy boutiques, used to be a route heavily trod by herds of cattle on their way to the grazing fields of Montauk? These are but two fascinating facts you'll learn as you tour the East Hampton area.

In order to do justice to each of the sites, though, it's important to pace yourself. East Hampton is a resort area as well as gold mine of historical artifacts; a journey into the past can be successfully combined with present-day indulgences, such as window-shopping and enjoying some of the marvelous food experiences.

Museums of East Hampton Historical Society Osborn-Jackson House, Clinton Academy, Town House And Mulford Farm

You can visit East Hampton viewing each of the individual museums, staffed by costumed interpreters, or by taking one of the lively, anecdote-filled tours given by Hugh King of the East Hampton Historical Society.

King goes by the name of the Town Crier, as much for his 19th-Century top-hatted attire as for his gift of well-informed gab. There are two tours given on Saturdays throughout the year, both of which meet at the Old Mulford House on James Lane.

The morning Cemetery Tour takes you through

Newsday Photo / Ari Mintz
The tools of Jackson Pollock and Lee Krasner

the Old Burying Ground, which dates back to about 1664. There, you'll see gravestones belonging to the likes of Lion Gardiner, one of the town's most prominent citizens, and Thomas James, East Hampton's first minister. The cemetery also is said to harbor the grave of Elizabeth Garlick, who, before the more famous Salem trials, went before a magistrate accused of witchcraft because a woman named Elizabeth Howell died shrieking her name. Also buried in that cemetery are 21 non-Hamptonites who perished in the shipwreck of the John Milton in 1859.

This tour also takes you to the meticulously preserved Mulford Farm, circa 1680 and Mulford Barn, circa 1721, you'll learn about the way people lived in the 17th and 18th Centuries. The museum is considered one of the most significant Colonial farms in America because it has all its original buildings in their original spots. It is also where you'll find Rachel's Garden, which won a National Garden Club Award. Here, too, you'll see examples of furniture made by the well known Dominy family.

On the afternoon tour, King visits several historic sites along Main Street, telling the stories of the people who built and inhabited them. You'll hear the history of the stagecoach that ran from Brooklyn to East Hampton, as well as the story of the Long Island Rail Road, originally built to get people to Greenport. Ask him to tell you the tales involving Aaron Burr.

You'll visit the Town House, which was built in 1731, and was the first town meeting house and school room. Here you can sit on a creaking bench at one of the old desks equipped with an inkpot and a quill.

At the Osborn-Jackson House, home of Sylvanus Mulford Osborn, a picture of 19th-Century family life emerges. There's the piano that Aunt Fanny played, the buttery and kitchen where generations of women cooked, and lots of furniture made by the Dominy family. The Dominy name is one you'll also come across many times on the East End, for not only were they a family of millwrights, but they were master furniture-makers. The study houses a wealth of old books, some of which still have stickers from the old East Hampton Library Co. Those interested in taxidermy might want to check out the display case filled with stuffed wildlife.

The Clinton Academy, now a museum, was built in 1784 by Samuel Buell, the town minister who also founded the East Hampton Library. Named for George Clinton, New York's first governor, the school was the first private school chartered after the American Revolution. In addition to changing exhibits, there's a Samuel Buell corner, with Buell's portrait next to the original chair and table depicted in the painting. You'll also see the clock and the weathervane from the original 1717 Puritan Church, which no longer exists but whose influence is still felt in the area.

Home Sweet Home

Take a break for lunch or a stroll through town before going on to the next attraction, the childhood residence of John Howard Payne, called "Home Sweet Home."

Payne is best known today for having written the words to the song of that name, which was an aria in the operetta "Clari" first performed in London in 1823. Payne was a true American Renaissance man, who wrote and published the first theatrical criticism in America at the age of 13, became a newspaper editor at 14, professionally

Directions

To East Hampton Historical Society Headquarters (in Osborn-Jackson House)
Take Route 27 (Montauk Highway) into East Hampton, where it becomes Main Street. Historical Society sites are before center of town, on the right.

To Clinton Academy (Town House next door)
Route 27 toward East Hampton. When road veers left, at the pond, continue to flag pole, turn right and go around; James Lane runs parallel to Montauk Highway across the pond.

To Home Sweet Home
Same as to Clinton Academy. Home Sweet Home is between St. Luke's Church and the Mulford Farm.

Pollock-Krasner House and Study Center
From East Hampton Village, continue east on Route 27 about a block to the Hook Windmill. Bear left just before windmill onto North Main Street, under railroad trestle. After three-quarters of a mile, take right fork marked Springs-Fireplace Road. Continue four miles, past Ashawagh Hall on right to 830 Fireplace Rd. on right.

Newsday Photo / Bill Davis
The door knocker at John Howard Payne's Home Sweet Home

produced an original five-act play at 18, and, in all, wrote more than 70 plays. Payne also was the first professional actor in America — our first Hamlet as well as our first Romeo. Having toured England and Ireland as an actor, he became the manager of the Sadler's Wells theater company.

A political activist, he was a staunch defender of American Indian rights. He also authored America's first copyright law.

The house itself, with the Pantigo windmill and beautiful garden on the property, was built in 1660; Payne may have been born there in 1791 (he claimed New York City in his autobiography). During this century, the house came into the hands of Mr. and Mrs. Gustav Buek of Brooklyn, who, between 1907 to 1927, put together a group of artifacts from Payne's lifetime.

There's a remarkable collection of lusterware, yellowware, blue Staffordshire china, and 19th-Century American furniture. You'll see, in the study, a carved chest that's the oldest piece of joined furniture made in America, and pretty Dominy chairs. Check out the clever mugs with little china frogs inside.

When Payne died in Tunis in 1852, while serving as American consul, Congress declared that he should not be buried on foreign soil. In 1883, America reclaimed this man for all seasons with a huge funeral in Washington, D.C., and a re-burial in Oak Hill Cemetery in Maryland.

Pollock-Krasner House And Study Center

East Hampton was also the adopted summer home of two other creative Americans, 20th Century abstract expressionist painters Jackson Pollock and Lee Krasner. Their home and studio, the Pollock-Krasner House, is a National Historic landmark property owned and operated by the State University at Stony Brook.

When you arrive, your guide will take you to the artists' studio, where you'll view a documentary exhibit on Pollock and Krasner. Then, you'll visit the house, which showcases two changing art exhibits a season.

Krasner and Pollock moved to the house on Accabonac Creek in 1945. It is there that Pollock, most famous for his "drip" paintings, worked until his death in 1956 when, at age 44, he was killed in an automobile accident while under the influence of alcohol. Krasner continued to work at the house in East Hampton during the summer almost until the end of her life in 1984.

When you visit the barn, which Pollock and Krasner converted into a studio, you have to take off your shoes and put on foam slippers so as not to damage the paint-splattered floor, considered an artifact. The room is filled with artists' equipment, but even more interesting is the exhibition of text and photographs that tell the story of the couple's life in East Hampton. Be sure to note the lesser-known domestic pictures, such as the charming photograph of Pollock with his pet crow.

The shingled house, built in 1879, is a small one, and when you visit their living quarters, it's hard not to feel as though you're trespassing on two very private lives. Intimate details are everywhere; Pollock's record collection, which demonstrates his keen interest in jazz. Upstairs, in Krasner's bedroom, are her necklaces and shell collection. Another room, now an office, was the studio Pollock used the first winter which, later, Krasner worked in while Pollock painted in the more spacious barn. A photo of the room in 1950 hangs there, affording a glimpse back. No, there aren't any major works of either artist on display in the barn or the house. What you'll get a rare opportunity to see, though, is an environment in which great creativity flourished.

Important Information

East Hampton Historical Society Headquarters (in Osborn-Jackson House)
101 Main St.
East Hampton
516-324-6850

Clinton Academy (Town House next door)
151 Main St.
  East Hampton

Mulford Farm
10 James Lane
East Hampton

Open: Spring and fall weekends, 10 a.m. to 5 p.m., July and August, seven days a week, from 10 a.m. to 5 p.m.; off-season by appointment
Fee: Each site $4 adults, $2 children, combined rates available
Tours: Town Crier, $10 per tour, call for hours.
Rest rooms: At all sites
On-site food: Information unavailable
Wheelchair access: Accessible
Gift shop: No, but small items for sale at individual sites
Child appropriate: Yes

Home Sweet Home
14 James Lane
East Hampton
516-324-0713

Open: April to December, 10 a.m. to 4 p.m., Monday to Saturday and 2 p.m. to 4 p.m. Sundays; closed holidays
Fee: $4 adults, $2 children
Tours: Yes
Rest rooms: No
On-site food: Information unavailable
Wheelchair access: No
Gift shop: Yes
Child appropriate: Older children

Pollock-Krasner House and Study Center
830 Fireplace Rd.
East Hampton
516-324-4929

Open: By appointment, May to October, Thursdays,

Fridays and Saturdays
Fee: $5 donation
Tours: Yes
Rest rooms: In house
On-site food: No
Wheelchair access: Partial; call ahead
Gift Shop: No
Child appropriate: Student tours can be arranged

Where to Eat

Turtle Crossing
221 Pantigo Rd.
East Hampton
516-324-7166
This nifty little barbecue joint and southwesterner is a couple of blocks past the town, but well worth the walk (or the short drive) for some marvelous smoky meat or else one of the imaginative wraps.

Golden Pear Cafe
34 Newtown Lane
East Hampton
516-329-1600
Great for a muffin and a cup of coffee, or else one of the swell sandwiches, this informal in-towner is a reasonably priced order-at-the-counter kind of place; still, an aura of Hamptons chic pervades.

Babette's
66 Newtown Lane
East Hampton
516-329-5377
At this lighthearted cafe, you can sit at one of the umbrella tables outdoors and watch the street scene, interesting in its own right. There are lots of vegetarian choices, and breakfast is truly special.

Rowdy Hall
10 Main St.
East Hampton
516-324-8555
A bit tricky to find, at the end of an alley directly across from the Main Street traffic light, this English pub-French bistro offers simple, well-executed classics, such as newspaper-wrapped fish and chips and fab burgers.

Della Femina
99 N. Main St.
East Hampton
516-329-6666
For dinner, if you want to splurge on some great New American fare, visit Jerry Della Femina's near-legendary people-watching hot spot.

AMAGANSETT AND MONTAUK

Long before Billy Joel called it home, Amagansett had a rich and interesting life of its own. How many of the summer people who flock there today know that during the 19th Century, Stephen Talkhouse, now a hot music club, was the nickname of a chatty Montaukett Indian named Stephen Pharaoh who took a legendary walk from Montauk to Brooklyn in one day? This was an area whose livelihood was dependent not upon tourism but upon whaling. Montauk, years from becoming a mecca for sport-fishing, surfing, and beach life, was known as the Wild West of the East — a destination dining spot for cattle herds on the munch. Ready for some heavy-duty time-tripping?

Marine Museum

Fittingly housed in a seaside cottage a mere clam shell's throw from the beach is the Amagansett Marine Museum. There, with some help from an East Hampton Historical Society guide, you'll wander amid artifacts depicting several hundred years of local maritime history. What you'll quickly realize is that although many families might not have been directly involved in harpooning whales, everyone in the region was, in one way or another, connected to the whaling industry.

On the wall along the staircase, you'll see photographs of prominent whaling families — the Edwards family, the Lester clan and the Bennetts. There are photographs of David Pharaoh, a Montaukett Indian involved in whaling, and of his

Newsday Photo / John H. Cornell Jr.
The essence of Long Island: The Montauk Lighthouse

kinsman, Stephen (Talkhouse) Pharaoh, who became famous for his one-day Brooklyn-to-Montauk walk as well as his gift of gab, and now the nightclub that bears his nickname. Then, there was the Dominy family, best known as furniture makers, who also were involved in the whaling industry and helped at lifesaving stations set up along the coastline to provide aid and rescue in case of shipwreck.

Upstairs, you'll see fascinating dioramas — one depicting trawling for cod, one explaining how the wetlands work as a renewable resource and yet another showing life under the bay. There's an exhibit entitled "Bayman's Year," which illustrates the different types of fish caught at different times. Throughout the museum, you'll see the artwork of the late Ray Prohaska, whose photographs and paintings vividly bring local maritime history to life.

The main room houses exhibits on shellfishing and eeling. There are boats everywhere — actual boats as well as models. Make sure to view the wall of shipwrecks, using illustrations, photographs and old maps to tell its sad stories. You'll learn about all the heroic work of those who assisted in the too-frequent times of distress. Don't forget to visit the basement, where you can see the cannon that came from the Culloden, which was shipwrecked in 1781 when it was grounded off Montauk Wells Point.

Throughout the museum, there are tons of whale-related paraphernalia: items fashioned of whale bone — corset stays and walking sticks — as well as some impressive scrimshaw work. You'll see harpoons, a huge skull of a fin whale, as well as a pointed-at-both-ends whaling boat. If you have the stomach for it, ask your guide what the phrases "Nantucket sleigh ride" and "fire on the chimneys" meant. It's hard not to become mesmerized by some of the more graphic 19th-Century photographs, especially the one depicting a whale being taken apart at a "cutting-in" party attended by what looks like the entire village.

Parents might want to check out the learning center, which involves youngsters in knot-making, games, books and puzzles relating to the sea. Outdoors, kids can enjoy the jungle gym made out of an old trawler.

Ramble about the back, where the boat collection includes a Dominy whale boat, the hundred-year-old Gil Smith catboat as well as some sharpies used by duck hunters. Wander into the old gunning shanty from the Indian Field Gun Club and imagine what it must have felt like to spend a night in such rustic surroundings before a pre-dawn duck hunt on the bay.

Miss Amelia Cottage Museum

In this quaint little white cottage, you'll discover three centuries in the life of one family. The house was built for Catherine Schellinger when she married John Conklin Jr. in 1725; it was moved to its present site in 1794. Its last occupant, Mary Amelia Schellinger — known as Miss Amelia — was born in the house in 1841 and lived there until her death in 1930.

From the outside, the house looks the way it did in 1850, but inside, each room is furnished to represent a different era of its past.

Downstairs, you'll see the large family room, with its beehive oven from 1725. Learn about how the earliest residents spun wool and made candles, how they drew water for cooking and bathing purposes. You'll also discover how the original paint in the downstairs bedrooms was uncovered and analyzed. One bedroom is a deep sage green. Then, there's the red "borning room" situated to catch the early eastern light. It is here that 30 Schellinger children were born, mostly during the early morning.

Back downstairs, you'll visit Miss Amelia's room which showcases some of the finest work of the locally

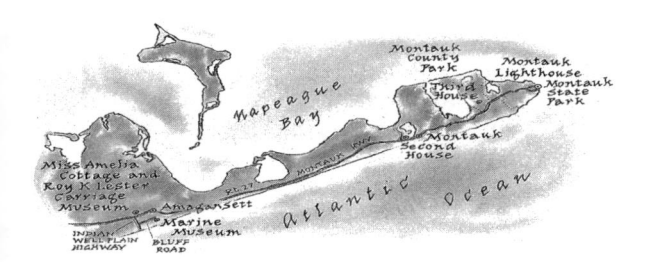

Directions

To Amagansett Marine Museum
Take Route 27 (Montauk Highway) east. Just before entering Village of Amagansett, make right at Mobil Station (Indian Well Plain Highway). Proceed to Bluff Road and make a left. Marine Museum is about a half-mile on right.

To Miss Amelia Cottage Museum and Roy K. Lester Carriage Museum
Route 27 (Montauk Highway) to Amagansett; museums are on north side just before town.

To Second House
Route 27 (Montauk Highway) eastbound; house is on left, half a block past Second House Road.

To Third House
Route 27 (Montauk Highway) past town; follow signs to Montauk County Park

To Montauk Lighthouse
Route 27 (Montauk Highway) past Montauk to end; follow signs to lighthouse.

---

famous Dominy family, especially known for their beautifully crafted furniture and clocks. Miss Amelia became the owner of one of the first oil stoves in Amagansett during the 1920s.

Roy K. Lester Carriage Museum

You don't have to travel far to find what has to be the niftiest collection of vintage carriages on the East End. They're housed right behind Miss Amelia's Cottage in the Richard H. Jackson Carriage House and the Roy K. Lester Barn.

First, at the Carriage House, you'll be charmed by the shiny turn-of-the-century Doctor's Buggy with its bright yellow wheels. Next to it is a 1953 photograph of original owner Dr. David Edwards and his bride, Carrie Mulford, riding on their 50th wedding anniversary. Other carriages invite the viewer to picture the vehicles in their heydays. Imagine the beautifully spindled beach wagon — known as a rockaway — transporting parties of summer bathers to the shore. You'll also see a gorgeous canopy-top surrey from 1910 as well as a wonderful 1895 Studebaker wagon.

A few steps away is the Roy K. Lester Barn, built in 1734 and moved to this site in 1979, when it was donated to the Amagansett Historical Association by Ruth and Mary Lester in memory of their brother Roy, an avid collector of carriages.

Among its many treasures are a rear-entry omnibus, a dandy collection of sleighs, and something called a "little speeding wagon," the horse-drawn equivalent of a sportscar.

Second House

Given its name, one might think that Second House was the second of three renowned cattle-keepers' houses to be built in Montauk (the first no longer exists, having been destroyed in a fire in 1909). Actually, it's really the *second* Second House — the first was built in 1746, to be replaced by this one in 1797. Enlarged at the beginning of the 19th Century, it was not only a refuge for cowboys but also an inn for those few wayfarers who made their way past the mosquito-infested Napeague stretch to Montauk, where they could hunt and fish.

The house, updated in 1990 by Victoria magazine, has a somewhat split personality. The upstairs rooms were decorated by the magazine in a Laura Ashley motif. But the first floor remains more authentic, showcasing some early American furniture belonging to the Kennedy family, who lived there from 1910 through the late 1950s. You'll see some Dominy pieces, a spinning wheel and, of course, a picture of the area's most famous Native American resident, the renowned Stephen (Talkhouse) Pharaoh. In the kitchen, you'll spot an 1891 ice cream maker.

Third House

Since the first Third House, erected in 1742, burned down, this structure — built in 1806 — is the second Third House. Currently part of the 1,059-acre Montauk County Park, the sprawling, rustic lodge is where Teddy Roosevelt and his Rough Riders camped out on their 1898 return from the Spanish American War. On the hilly grounds, the troops took time to recover from war wounds and

Newsday Photo / Thomas A. Ferrara
A whaling boat at the Marine Museum in Amagansett

tropical illnesses before mustering out.

While the building, which is currently under renovation (call to check if it's opened) holds little more than some old photographs of T.R. and his men, it can be fascinating to look out on the property and envision the men the way they appeared when caught on camera. There's also a great shot of Roosevelt's pet lioness, Josephine.

Montauk Lighthouse

Here, at the lighthouse, a small but sophisticated museum in the adjoining lightkeeper's house is home to a priceless collection of photographs and memorabilia dating back to the structure's beginnings. First commissioned in 1792, the lighthouse wasn't actually lit until 1797. Although renovated in 1860, the original base from Washington's era still remains.

In the first room of the museum — the lightkeeper's parlor — you'll find not only a visual history of the various lighthouse keepers but a wealth of drawings, architectural blueprints, and photographs of the lighthouse between 1791 and 1939. The room's centerpiece is the original commissioning document complete with Thomas Jefferson's signature.

The adjoining room, which once functioned as the lightkeeper's bedroom, is named in honor of Georgina Reid, who devised a terracing method to stop the erosion of the bluff on which the lighthouse is perched. A series of dioramas graphically depict the progress of beach erosion.

In the central hallway is a marvelous exhibit entitled "Lighthouses Surrounding Long Island." Here, on a huge model board, you'll find miniatures of all the lighthouses from Manhattan to Rhode Island. A push of a button enables you to light up the lighthouse of your choice and read about its history.

There's also a room showcasing the actual lenses and lamps employed throughout the lighthouse's long history. Of course, no trip to the lighthouse is complete without the 137-step climb to the top. During World War II, the coastline surrounding the lighthouse (which became a Coast Guard station in 1938) was heavily fortified against possible German submarine invasion. Look southward and you'll see some of the remnants of Camp Hero, part of the Eastern Coastal Defense Shield. An old radar tower remains from where the Air Force base once was.

Important Information

Amagansett Marine Museum
Bluff Road
Amagansett
516-324-6850

Open: Daily, 10 a.m. to 5 p.m. July and August; Weekends in spring and fall 10 a.m. to 5 p.m.; other times by appointment.
Fee: $4, $2 children and seniors
Tours: Yes
Rest rooms: upstairs
On-site food: None, but there are picnic tables in back
Wheelchair access: Partial
Gift shops: No
Child appropriate: Yes

Miss Amelia Cottage Museum and Roy K. Lester Carriage Museum
Montauk Highway at Windmill Lane
Amagansett
516-267-3020

Open: Memorial Day to Labor Day, Friday to Sunday, 10 a.m. to 4 p.m.
Fee: $2 adults; $1 children
Tours: Yes
Rest rooms: Yes, in the barn
On-site food: No
Wheelchair access: Limited; call for details
Gift shop: No
Child appropriate: Yes

Second House
Montauk Highway
Montauk
516-668-5340

Open: Daily, 10 a.m. to 4 p.m. Memorial Day to Columbus Day
Fee: $2; $1 under 12
Tours: Informal
Rest rooms: No
On-site food: No
Wheelchair access: No
Gift Shop: Yes
Child appropriate: Somewhat

Third House
Montauk County Park
Montauk
516-852-7878

Open: 8 a.m. to 4 p.m. daily Memorial Day to Labor Day; then weekends to Oct. 31; other times by appointment.
Fee: Free
Tours: No
Rest rooms: Yes
On-site food: No, but there are picnic facilities in park
Wheelchair access: Information not available
Gift Shop: No
Child appropriate: Older children

Montauk Lighthouse
Montauk State Park
516-668-2544
Open: 10:30 a.m. to 4 p.m. Monday to Saturday; 2 p.m. to 4 p.m. Sunday
Fee: $3; $1 ages 6-12
Tours: Self-guided
Rest rooms: Not on property; in the adjacent State Park
On-site food: No
Wheelchair access: Only to main level museum
Gift shop: Yes
Child appropriate: Yes

Where to Eat

Estia
177 Main St.
Amagansett
516-267-6320
This unpretentious-looking cafe is a fine breakfast

or lunch option. It's at dinner, though, that the menu really shines. It ranges from homemade pasta to exotic game, with produce grown in the chef's vegetable and herb garden.

The Lobster Roll
1980 Montauk Hwy. (Napeague Stretch)
Amagansett
516-267-3740
Justly renowned for its world-famous lobster roll, this wildly popular seafood stop offers lots more. There are all manner of fish sandwiches, some fried, others grilled, as well as fresh seafood specialties. Come early, though, because there's usually a long wait.

Cyril's Fish House
2167 Montauk Hwy. (Napeague Stretch)
Amagansett
516-267-7933
There's almost always a young, hip crowd at this cute Carribean-looking fish house. The lobster roll is marvelous, and the other seafood specialties are more than respectable.

Bird on the Roof
47 S. Elmwood Ave.
Montauk
516-668-5833
Housed in a beachy boutique, this funky little indoor-outdoor cafe offers some of the best breakfast and lunch deals on the East End. The creative omelets are unforgettable, the French toast is grand, and the sandwiches aren't bad, either. Best of all, you'll leave with change in your pockets.

The Harvest on Fort Pond
11 S. Emory St.
Montauk
516-668-5574
This serene dinner-only spot is where you might want to reward yourself after a long day of touring. Although prices are high, much of the well-prepared eclectic-Italianate fare serves more than one, so think in terms of large groups. Romantics will revel in the views of Fort Pond Bay.

SAG HARBOR: THE WHALING LIFE

If you were to ask the average American citizen of 200 years ago to name the nation's great ports, you'd probably hear Sag Harbor mentioned in the same breath as New York City. That's because one of the first acts passed by Congress was the establishment of New York City and "Sagg-harbour" as one of the state's two official U.S. Ports of Entry.

Clearly, things have changed. What was once a thriving center for foreign trade and whaling has become a quaint summer resort village — a fine spot to shop and to dine, but hardly a major hub for international commerce. Yet all is not lost from those glory days. Sag Harbor is still home to a wealth of landmark buildings whose architectural styles trace the development of the town.

Architecture buffs can view this site among others detailed on a walking tour pamphlet put out by the Society for the Preservation of Long Island Antiquities, which owns the Sag Harbor Custom House. You can pick one up with the tour at the Custom House or write for it at the society at 93 N. Country Rd., Setauket, N.Y., 11733-1350. We'll concentrate on the interiors of three Sag Harbor landmarks. Combine that with a stroll through the village, and it's a full day's outing.

Newsday Photo / Bill Davis

In front of the Custom House, a Nathaniel Dominy V round dishtop table made in 1792 from a single piece of mahogany.

The Custom House

Why, you might wonder, is the old Custom House of Sag Harbor located in a gracious homestead rather than in an official-looking edifice filled with offices and waiting rooms? It's because when Henry Packer Dering was named Sag Harbor's custom master in 1789, he chose to conduct federal business in his comfortable private dwelling. It was under that same roof that he also managed to raise nine children. One of those children, Henry Thomas Dering, became custom master after his father, so, in all, the Dering family occupied the Custom House for sixty years, until 1849. By that time, Sag Harbor was a major center for the whaling industry.

One could dub the Sag Harbor Custom House the Long Island answer to Monticello — a modest answer, to be sure, but still a rather imposing one for the area. The house is a center-hall Colonial with two large rooms on either side and a kitchen in the back. That kitchen offers an idea of life during the 18th Century, with its large cooking hearth and little sitz-tub for sponge bathing.

The Dering name was a prominent one; Shelter Island's Dering Harbor, where the family originally had their home, was named for Henry Packer Dering's father. During the Revolution, while the Derings temporarily took refuge in Connecticut, Henry went to Yale for his education. His 1784 diploma is on display downstairs, along with the original document establishing Sag Harbor as a port.

Much of the furniture in the house — like the Newport eight-day clock made by William Claggert — came from Dering's father's Shelter Island home. Many of the rooms are painted in the original bright colors so popular during Dering's day. Upstairs, bedroom walls are hung with reproduction wallpaper representative of the era. Folks then, it seemed, liked to mix patterns with near-abandon.

Before you leave, close your eyes a moment and try to envision the house as it must have been during Dering's lifetime, when the transaction of major national business and the tumult of nine growing children co-existed under one roof.

The Sag Harbor Whaling And Historical Museum

The inscription over the pediment of the beautiful wooden Greek Revival building that houses the Sag Harbor Whaling Museum reads "Masonic Temple," but originally, there was no such inscription. The building, designed by Minard LeFever of New York City, was erected in 1845 as the private home of Benjamin Huntting, a whaling ship captain and shipowner. After Huntting's death, the edifice was owned by Mrs. Russell Sage and, after her death, it was bought by the local Masonic Lodge. The lodge ultimately decided to deed the building to the town for a whaling museum, but they retained privileges to hold meetings upstairs, which they still do.

It's downstairs that you'll be touring — after entering through the jawbones of a right whale. The first few rooms, to your left, called the Sag Harbor Rooms, showcase an assortment of memorabilia that, collectively, chronicle the life in the town. There are early paintings of children done by itinerant limners as well as a beautiful 19th-Century wedding gown. A collection of the great sailing ships of the world, fashioned out of sterling silver, is particularly interesting, as is an 1860 tricycle. Next door is a roomful of antique toys. There's an awesomely realistic model of the Hell Gate Bridge as well as an enormous celestial globe, made in 1836 by astronomer Ephram Niles Byram. In addition to a nifty old piano, you'll find an arrowhead collection, an antique sewing machine, a typewriter and an entire

Directions

To The Custom House
Long Island Expressway to exit 70 south to Sunrise Highway. Head east on Sunrise through Southampton, where it joins with Montauk Highway. Continue eastward to Bridgehampton. Turn left at the war monument onto the Bridgehampton-Sag Harbor Turnpike. Continue into the Village of Sag Harbor, turning left on Garden Street.

Sag Harbor Whaling Museum
Next door to The Custom House

Sag Harbor Fire Department Museum
Walk from The Custom House toward the harbor along Main Street to Sage Street, walk one block to corner of Church Street.

---

wall of old guns. There's also a display honoring William Wallace Tooker, who studied the language and lore of the local Indians.

In an adjoining room, you'll find a replica of an

The Sag Harbor Whaling Museum, which was built in 1845
Newsday Photo / John H. Cornell Jr.

18th-Century kitchen. Check out the early version of a washing machine as well as the old map of Sag Harbor that hangs on the wall. Next, you'll come to a room displaying the implements used by whaling ship captains. Here, you'll find some neat models of schooners, a shield from Borneo and a harpoon gun.

The last room is the most artistically riveting, with its collection of old pianos unlike most. Take time to admire the intricately carved draft piano made in Baltimore in 1868 and the rare Giraffe piano that has only 84 rather than 88 keys. There's also a sculpture collection and an assortment of canes, many of them fashioned of whalebone.

Before you leave, walk to the center of the hall and look straight up at the beautiful oval spiral staircase. At the top is a dome with a stained-glass skylight, a graceful reminder of a graceful era.

Sag Harbor Fire Department Museum

Back when our nation was new, Sag Harbor was a town in the forefront of progress. So it shouldn't be surprising that the Sag Harbor Fire Department is the oldest volunteer department in the state. The department was commissioned in 1803 by the State Legislature (you can see the original minutes of the session in the museum), and, in 1896, took up residence in this building, built in 1836, which doubled as village hall and Sunday school room. The building remained in active use until the fire department moved its headquarters downtown in 1976. Two years later, on the Sag Harbor Fire Department's 175th anniversary, volunteers

restored the building as a museum.

And a quirky and fascinating museum it is — it houses two antique hand-pulled fire carts, the building's original stove, as well as a lot of old equipment, like a bull-horn through which the fire chief shouted directions to his men. You'll learn about how an airhorn told volunteer firefighters — in code — exactly where each fire was.

On a back wall is a huge mural depicting two major fires in Sag Harbor, one in 1915 and the other on New Year's Eve, 1925. Both these events were recorded in photographs, displayed so that you can compare them to the painting.

There's lots for kids to do — wind up the fire alarm and make a lot of noise, and pull the bell upstairs. On the way up those stairs, note the photographs of local teams dating to the late 19th Century. On the second level, you'll find an assortment of antiquities — old trophies, antique toy fire-trucks, and a drum that once belonged to the village band. There's also a huge collection of patches from various fire departments as well as a replica of a drying tower, where linen hoses were aired out to prevent them from rotting.

Back downstairs, pause at the odd little gift shop where anyone who wants can see, and even buy, a videotape of Sag Harbor's downtown big fire of 1994. Curious viewing, indeed.

Important Information

The Custom House
Main and Garden Streets
Sag Harbor
516-941-9444

Open: June and September, Saturday and Sunday, 10 a.m. to 4 p.m.; July and August, Tuesday to Sunday, 10 a.m. to 5 p.m.
Fee: $3; $1.50 ages 7-14 and over 60
Tours: Yes
Rest rooms: No; use Whaling Museum next door
On-site food: No
Wheelchair access: No
Gift shop: No
Child appropriate: Yes

Sag Harbor Whaling Museum
Main and Garden Streets
Sag Harbor
516-725-0770

Open: May 15 to Sept. 30, Monday to Saturday, 10 a.m. to 5 p.m.; Sunday, 1 p.m. to 5 p.m.

Fee: $3; $1 ages 6 to 13, $2 over 60
Tours: Information unavailable
Rest rooms: Yes
On-site food: No
Wheelchair access: Yes
Gift shop: Yes
Child appropriate: Yes

Sag Harbor Fire Department Museum
Sage and Church Streets
Sag Harbor
516-725-0779

Open: July 4th through Labor Day, noon to 4 p.m. daily
Fee:: $1 adults, $50 children, under 10, free
Tours: Information unavailable
Rest rooms: Yes
On-site food: Information unavailable
Wheelchair access: No
Gift shop: Yes
Child appropriate: Yes

Where to Eat

La Superica
Main Street (foot of bridge)
516-725-3388
The California-style Mexican fare is sprightly and interesting, the salsa fresh and vibrant at this colorful little cantina. If you come in the evening and plan to catch a sunset with an early dinner, know that the bouncy 20-something crowd often gets quite noisy.

Paradise Diner
126 Main St.
516-725-6080
A popular breakfast spot for many, this recently refurbished diner serves some interesting upscale items come lunch and dinnertime. Although the fare is right on target, the prices in the evening are typically Hamptonesque.

Java Nation
Main Street (in a little courtyard)
516-725-0500
At this hip yet charming little coffee-and-a-nosh cafe, they not only grind a variety of fresh coffee beans; they also roast them on premises. Consequently, the coffee here is better even than that at you-know-which Seattle-based chain. Try a java, a capuccino, or a latte. Their espresso is about as intense and as good as it gets. Baked goods are homey and delicious.

THE NORTH FORK

A serene and picturesque respite from the malls and the expressway, Long Island's North Fork offers its own quiet enticements. The burgeoning wine-growing industry that has grown up here over the past two decades is a source of fierce regional pride, so when you're in the area, do try to work at least one winery into your itinerary. (See the list on Page 159.)

Our tour begins in Southold and ends in Orient, but along the way you can ramble about any of the pretty communities you pass in between. And don't forget to stop at a roadside farmstand en route home.

Historical Museums of Southold

The museum grounds are spread out over Main Road in quaint Southold. The historic Prince Building is home to the administrative office, the museum archives, as well as a charming gift shop. A block away are the major restorations.

Start there, at the Victorian residence that was the home of writer and historian Ann Currie-Bell. Built by her father, Joseph Hallock in 1900, the house incorporates a number of architectural and decorative styles. If you're an aficionado of period costumes and hats, you'll find a treasure trove here.

In the front parlor, look up at the ceiling to admire the beautiful gold leaf-trimmed painting of the sky. On the wall of the parlor is a portrait of Hallock, who was the Southold town clerk, assemblyman, and owner of the newspaper. Note the excellent condition of the Victorian furniture here and throughout the house. The Victorian kitchen is a sight indeed, with its old-fashioned range, ice box and water pump; not to mention a doughnut maker, a coffee grinder, a cherry pitter, and a dandy old telephone.

Newsday Photo / Bill Davis

An anchor from a wreck frames the Horton Point Lighthouse

It was while traveling though the French countryside that Ann Hallock — then in her 30s — first saw the Scottish artist Thomas Currie-Bell, a widower 20 years her senior, at work on a painting. She stopped to admire the canvas, and a relationship began. Currie-Bell followed Ann home and shortly thereafter, the two were married.

An entire upstairs room of the house is devoted to the Currie-Bells' romance. In addition to being a renowned portraitist and landscape painter with one work hanging in the Hermitage in St. Petersburg, Thomas Currie-Bell was also a musician, a sailor, and a composer. The sheet music to a love song he composed for the woman he called ''Nannie'' is on display in that room, as is the painting Ann admired when the two first met.

Also upstairs is a fascinating doll collection in Ann's childhood bedroom, as well as a unique dollhouse her aunt fashioned out of soap boxes. Move on to the sewing room and check out some of the grand vintage clothing — a petticoat made especially for bicycling, a duster used for motoring, and a dress with an early Saks Fifth Avenue label. And, oh, those hats! Be sure to see the bathroom, innovative for its time, with its pull-chain toilet and old shaving mugs. In the master bedroom, stop to admire the lovely quilt, the fine woodwork, and the old family photographs on the wall.

Outdoors, stroll over to the beautiful, raftered 18th-Century barn. Inside, you'll find an impressive collection of sleighs, sleds and carriages, including an 1870 sleigh used specifically to deliver groceries. One section of the barn is devoted to pigs: there's a sausage-stuffer, lard press, meat-chopping block, hock scraper, as well as a graphic photograph of a hog being butchered by members of the Currie-Bell family.

Explore the outbuildings: the little circular icehouse, the buttery, the corn crib, a farm machine building, and a print shop. And don't miss the pink jewel-box of a millinery, with its flowered curtains. There's even an old privy, restored for public use. The 1822 Bayview schoolhouse is furnished with ink-well-equipped wooden desks and an old wood-burning stove. Browse through the old books. Nearby, you'll find a blacksmith shop, operational until 1940.

On the property, you'll also find one of the most interesting old buildings on Long Island, the Thomas Moore House, named for the original settler on whose land the Landon family built their home in 1750. Infused with the fragrance of antiquity, the house is painted in the original blues and greens used during the 18th Century. A hearth with a simulated fire illuminates the "keeping room," where most family life took place.

A kitchen, added 100 years later, now showcases a prized loom. Off the front hall is an elegant parlor with a fine collection of lusterware in an old hutch.

The master bedroom, outfitted with a cradle and an additional trundle bed, was not only for ma and pa, but also a place for the youngest children to sleep before they were old enough for the attic bedrooms. A tiny room next to the fire was well-suited for use as a sickroom.

There's a surprise at the top of the very narrow staircase, where an extraordinary doll collection is on display, that can take you on a journey through history. You'll see early models, one fashioned out of a blanket tied with a ribbon, another made of sticks.

Horton Point Lighthouse

In a beautiful parklike setting, this 140-year-old lighthouse with a small museum overlooks the Long Island Sound.

In that museum, you'll find a collection of

Directions

To Historic Museums at Southold
Long Island Expressway east to end. Go east on Route 25 through several towns, passing two traffic lights in Cutchogue. In Southold, just before the Maple Lane light on the northwest side near the bank, you'll find the Prince Building. The buildings are past the traffic light on the southeast side.

To Horton Point Lighthouse
From Museums at Southold, go west on Route 25, turn right onto Youngs Avenue, proceed to where road ends at North Road, take quick right and left onto Lighthouse Road. Follow signs.

To Oysterponds Historical Society Museum
East on Route 25 past Greenport and East Marion until you reach the monument at Village Lane. Turn right and continue to museum complex on left.

---

whaling tools and lighthouse artifacts from centuries past. Of particular note is a collection of ships' records and memorabilia brought back from the voyages of several East End whaling captains. Take time to admire the portrait of Capt. Henry Green, and examine the beautiful printed silk baby quilt from Japan, an 1846 gift from Capt. Mercator Cooper to his sister-in-law, Henry Green's wife, Roxana. Among other treasures are a collection of 18th-Century "pieces of eight" used as currency in the colony. There's an old chandler's safe, an assortment of submarine artifacts, some whale oil lamps, a battleship model, and scrimshaw work done by those who worked at the lifesaving stations that dotted the coastline. You also can see the first

The music room in The Village House, built in 1798 by Augustus Griffin, who ran it as a stagecoach stop and inn.

geographic map of the Long Island Sound, printed in 1855. A serendipitous item — discovered under the rug of the original lighthouse keeper's dwelling — is an original newspaper printed two days after Lincoln's assassination.

In a room downstairs, original oil paintings make naval history come to life. There's also a model of the whale ship Morgan under full sail, on loan from the American Oceanographic Society. Pause for a moment near a small but important exhibit about Horton Point's first woman lighthouse keeper, Stella Prince. The museum connects by a breezeway to the lighthouse itself, one of the only three lighthouse towers accessible to the public on Long Island. No trip would be complete without the steep, winding climb to the top. Observe the gargoyles surrounding the outside of the tower; most are made from casts of the originals, which were damaged by vandals. The view from the top is magnificent.

Oysterponds Historical Society

Not far from the tip of the North Fork is this remarkable collection of old buildings which collectively chronicle over 200 years of village life.

The Old Point Schoolhouse, built in 1888, houses the administrative offices, a gallery for changing exhibits and a research library — open only by appointment — where one of Long Island's largest collections of documents and primary sources is kept.

Next door is The Village House, built in 1798 by Augustus Griffin, a Southold Town historian who ran it as a stagecoach stop and inn. In 1853, it was bought by the Vail family, who renovated it and, during the 1880s, converted it into a boarding house. It is in that Victorian boardinghouse motif that the site has been refurbished. One can only imagine the meals boarders shared around the imposing dining room tables. Upstairs are six bedrooms, three furnished to reflect the boardinghouse era, one used as an exhibit on Civil War memorabilia, and another a display room for trunks.

In the nearby Hallock Building, which was built in 1891 and moved in 1961 from the Hallock Farm, you'll find an exhibit on maritime culture. In addition to scrimshaw, you can see a fine collection of portraits of trading schooners and steamships. There's a fascinating exhibit on East End whaling, where you'll see the journals kept by Edwin Brown, a whaler who lived in Orient. Even more interesting are the journals and diary kept by his wife, Martha Smith Brewer Brown, one of the few women to accompany her husband to sea.

Conclude your visit at the Webb House, built in the Federalist style of the 18th Century. Believed to have first been a tavern, the house was moved from Greenport to its present location several decades ago. The summer and winter kitchens have been restored to their their original celery green and russet colors; the parlor is quite stiff and formal. Upstairs, the inn-style bedrooms are furnished just the way an 18th-Century wayfarer might have found them.

Important Information

Historic Museums at Southold
Main Road and Maple Lane
Southold
516-765-5500

Open: July 4th to mid-September; Wednesday, Saturday, Sunday, 1 p.m. to 4 p.m.
Fee: Suggested donation $1.50, children, 50 cents
Tours: Yes
Rest rooms: Yes
On-site food: No
Wheelchair access: Downstairs only, in Currie-Bell House
Gift shop: Yes
Child appropriate: Yes

Horton Point Lighthouse
Lighthouse Road
Southold
516-765-5500

Open: Memorial Day Weekend to Columbus Day weekend, Saturday and Sunday from 11:30 a.m. to 4

p.m., other times by appointment for schools and special groups
Fee: Children free, donations suggested, $2
Tours: As needed
Rest rooms: Yes
On-site food: No
Wheelchair access: Only museum
Gift shop: Yes
Child appropriate: Yes

Oysterponds Historical Society Museum
Village Lane
Orient
516-323-2480

Open: June through September, Tuesday, Saturday and Sunday, 2 p.m. to 5 p.m. and other times by appointment.
Fee: $3 adults; 50 cents children under 12; members free
Tours: Yes
Rest rooms: Yes
On-site food: No
Wheelchair access: No
Gift shop: In Village House
Child appropriate: Yes

Where to Eat

Jamesport Country Kitchen
Main Road
Jamesport
516-722-3537
On your way out, stop for lunch at this gracious little storefront cafe, where the fare is fresh and imaginatively done. Try a sandwich on focaccia scented with rosemary — the salmon cake is a winner, as is the grilled chicken with pesto. For dinner, on the way back, savor such Long Island specialties as herbal clam chowder, a locally caught tuna steak with mango salsa, and roast duck with a pear-walnut-cranberry relish. A slice of fruit tart makes for a fitting lovely conclusion.

Hellenic Snack Bar
Main Road
East Marion
516-477-0138
In the summer, you can dine outdoors in an arborlike setting at this well-established standby for well-prepared Greek food. The wood fired rotisserie is always ablaze, turning out wonderful grilled marinated meats — souvlaki, skewered chicken, lamb. Homemade lemonade, incidentally, is legendary.

MAJOR THOMAS JONES' ISLAND

To imagine a Long Island without a Jones Beach would be to fancy a Paris without an Eiffel Tower. Yet before 1929, Jones Beach, as we know it today, simply didn't exist. How did the recreational facility so many people take for granted come to be? And exactly who was Maj. Thomas Jones, the man for whom it was named? Take this two-part tour, and you'll find the answers to these questions. And more.

Old Grace Church Complex (Historical Society of the Massapequas)

"**O**ur Major Jones" is the term used by members of the Historical Society of the Massapequas when referring to the illustrious and colorful Maj. Thomas Jones, who came to this country in the late 17th Century and helped shape the destiny of Long Island. Jones lies buried in the cemetery behind the Old Grace Church, part of a three-building complex that also encompasses The Delancey Floyd-Jones Free Library and the Elbert Floyd-Jones Servants' Cottage.

Although the complex is small, plan on spending at least a couple of hours here. Tours are by appointment, which is definitely worth making since your guide will have some detailed and fascinating stories to tell.

Start with the Delancey Floyd-Jones Library, built in 1896 by the man whose portrait hangs in the stately oak-appointed main room. Delancey Floyd-Jones, a descendant of Maj. Thomas Jones, was a Civil War hero and wealthy world traveler who wrote about his journeys abroad. Childless but not rootless, he built this library for the children of Massapequa.

Currently, the library functions as a research

The Castles in the Sand exhibit at Jones Beach

Newsday Photo / David L. Pokress

facility whose focus is the history of Long Island. On its shelves is an autobiography signed by Helen Keller and a travelogue autographed by Theodore Roosevelt. Children will be particularly enchanted by some of the old series in the back room — the Bobbsey Twins, the Hardy Boys, and Cherry Ames, to name a few. What's truly remarkable is that the library and all its furnishings are in their original state; a photograph taken when the library opened attests to this.

On one wall, you'll see a painting of the Floyd-Jones House that stood in Oyster Bay until 1934. This was an early home of Maj. Thomas Jones.

Jones, a proponent of King James II of England, fled Europe for political reasons and became a privateer — a sort of gentleman pirate.

After losing his ship in an earthquake in Jamaica, Jones struck out for America in 1692. There, he met and married a young woman named Freelove Townsend, daughter of Rhode Island privateer Thomas Townsend.

What did the new father-in-law give the couple for a wedding present? Massapequa. He'd acquired it in a business deal with local Indians years earlier. (At least that's the most romantic version of how Jones acquired his land.)

Initially, Thomas and Freelove lived in Oyster Bay before moving to Massapequa to build what would be the first brick house on Long Island's South Shore. Their fortunes flourished; Jones became a warden of Church of England, the first supervisor of the Town of Oyster Bay, and ranger general of Long Island. After learning much about whaling from the American Indians who lived nearby, he established the first whaling station on what is now Jones Beach. As ranger general, Jones owed some of his haul to the then-regional Governor Cornsbury. Ask your guide to tell you some of the more colorful stories relating to Cornsbury.

When Jones died, at age 53, he owned 6,000 acres

on Long Island and had seven children. One of his sons, David, stipulated in his will that any female in the family wishing to inherit property would have to affix the name Jones to her husband's name. That is how, when David's daughter Arabella married Richard Floyd, cousin of William Floyd (Long Island's signer of the Declaration of Independence), the Floyd-Jones family name was born.

When you move on to the Elbert Floyd-Jones Cottage, you'll learn that this modest 1880 building started out as servants quarters on the estate of its namesake, which was originally located behind what is now the Bar Harbor Library.

During the 1920s, the cottage was home to the Gottert family, whose pictures you'll see on the parlor wall. In that room, you'll also find a pump-operated parlor organ, a beautiful old Singer sewing machine, and a coal-burning stove original to the house.

A pump sink, a stove that used bottled gas, and a fine old ice chest are in the kitchen. There's an exhibit room showcasing photographs of old Massapequa, with its mansions and fine hotels as well as old family portraits.

Next on your itinerary is the lovely Old Grace Church, erected in 1844. Episcopal by denomination, it was originally designed in the Greek Revival style but, around the turn of the century, was remodeled as a Carpenter Gothic church.

Inside, there's a stained glass altar window depicting Jesus talking to four disciples in a waterside scene, evoking the congregation's South Shore locale. The church is characterized by graceful Gothic arches and quatrefoil and fleur-de-lis motifs.

It was deconsecrated several years ago when a larger house of worship was built across the street; that's where all the original side-windows are today. The replacements you see came from a New Jersey church of the same age. The church retains its original pews, baptismal font, light fixtures (electrified now), as well as the cross above the altar, a gift from Delancey Floyd-Jones.

Walk outside and you'll come, first, to a charming little cemetery that's open to the public for burial. Beyond that is the private Floyd-Jones cemetery, entered through a canopylike structure called a lych-gate.

Here, you'll find the graves of Major Thomas Jones and his wife, Freelove. Although Jones had originally been buried in another part of Massapequa, he was moved here during the 19th Century.

People, it seemed, kept digging him up, motivated by the assumption (erroneous, it turned out) that a former privateer would have been buried with his treasure.

There are other noteworthy graves, as well:

Directions

**To Massapequa Historical Society
(Old Grace Church and cemetery,
Delancey-Floyd Jones Library,
Elbert-Floyd-Jones Cottage)**
Southern State Parkway to exit 29 south; take
Hicksville Road south to Merrick Road; turn left. The
complex is about three-fourths of a mile on left.

To Castles in the Sand
Wantagh or Meadowbrook Parkway to Jones Beach;
follow signs to Field 6; East Bathhouse is nearby.

Richard Floyd-Jones, first to be born with the
hyphenated version of the family name, and his wife,
Sarah Onderdonk Floyd-Jones, as well as George
Stanton Floyd-Jones, who owned a mansion where
Massapequa High School now stands.

And, yes, Delancey Floyd-Jones reposes here, too.

A quick side-trip: On your way to Jones Beach,
heading west on Merrick Road, you'll pass the Jones
cemetery, which has its own historical marker.

Ask your guide from the Historical Society of the
Massapequas for exact directions, as well as for
instructions on finding the grave of Kezia Youngs
Jones.

She is remembered as the young girl George
Washington kissed on his way out of her father's
home. The 17-year-old swore she'd never again
wash her face. A few months later, she married
William Jones, a great-grandson of Maj. Thomas
Jones.

Jones Beach
(Castles in the Sand)

A bright afternoon on a weekend neither too hot nor too cold is ideal for this tour, which should begin or end with a bracing stroll on the boardwalk.

The wonderful nostalgia-filled exhibit entitled "Castles in the Sand" is housed in the East Bathhouse between Field 6 and the Golf Course. Here, you'll learn not only about the origins of Jones Beach State Park, but about Long Island's other state parks and its parkways. Appropriately, the first room is dominated by a photographic portrait of Robert Moses, the visionary president of the Long Island State Parks Commission between 1924 and 1966.

Although Moses was a controversial figure, it was he who pioneered the idea of a parkway — literally, a road leading to a park. In Moses' view, though, a parkway was not merely a road but rather miles and miles of parklands which contained a road, engineered purely for pleasurable motoring. You'll see a wonderful 1934 photograph from the Brooklyn Eagle entitled, "Long Island, the Motorist's Paradise," depicting the rustic bridges along the Southern State Parkway. Another photo shows bridge construction along the Northern State Parkway in 1937. But parkways came at some expense, as we see by looking at a snapshot of a house being moved in 1953 for the expansion of Southern State.

To get an overview of the wealth of state parks on Long Island, check out the chart outlining their development. Then, enjoy some of the vintage photographs on display. There's the old ski tow and the elegant Lenox Room clubhouse at Bethpage State Park. You'll also find a marvelous 1940 photo-tryptych depicting ice skating at Belmont Lake State Park, plus architectural drawings of the Sunken Meadow bathhouse made in 1921, as well as elevations of the since-replaced 1931 Colonial Revival bathhouse at Heckscher State Park.

But the true star is Jones Beach itself. You'll see photographic documentation of how it was created, using 40 million cubic yards of sand pumped from the inlet that would become Zach's Bay. There also are photos of High Hill Beach, the community supplanted by the creation of the state park. You can follow the construction of Ocean Parkway as well as the building of the water tower, now a landmark.

An immense blowup of a calisthenics class during the '30s dominates the main room of the exhibit. Artifacts from bygone days abound;

there's a snapshot of the old Marine Dining Room, as well as a menu dated May 28, 1938: "Dinner for today — $1.25." A sign reads, "Afternoon tea-dancing daily from 4 p.m. to 6 p.m.; $.50 per person." There's even a photo of a playground for *adults*, circa 1940.

Photographs of the original 1931 stadium in Zach's Bay depict a floating stage for "music over the water and under the stars" (the current stadium was built in 1952). In keeping with the park's marine theme, all Jones Beach employees were dressed in nautical attire; fittingly, staff members at today's exhibit wear sailor suits.

Old newsreels run continuously on a video screen. One, entitled "Beauty and the Beach" opens an enthralling window to an era when children's games were held in Princess Rosebud's teepee. Another, entitled "By the Sea," depicts water ballets under sunny skies and dancing under the stars at the beach's outdoor nightclub.

Important Information

Historical Society of the Massapequas (Old Grace Church and Cemetery, Delancey-Floyd Jones Library, Elbert-Floyd-Jones Cottage)
4755 Merrick Rd.
Massapequa
516-541-5337

Open: Church open 2 p.m. to 4 p.m. Sundays from Memorial Day to Columbus Day; other buildings as well as church, year-round by appointment only.
Fee: Free
Tours: Yes
Rest rooms: In old church
On-site food: No
Wheelchair access: No
Gift shop: No
Child appropriate: Yes

Castles in the Sand
East Bathhouse, Jones Beach
516-785-1600

Open: Year-round, weekends 10 a.m. to 4 p.m.; Memorial Day to mid-October, daily noon to 8 p.m.
Fee: $1, children under 42 inches tall, free
Tours: Self-guided
Rest rooms: On east side of building
On-site food: At various spots on the beach
Wheelchair access: Yes
Gift shop: In central mall, Field 4

Child appropriate: Yes

Where to Eat

Butera's
4964 Merrick Rd. (Southgate Center)
Massapequa Park
516-795-1929
or
Cafe Butera
4958 Merrick Rd. (Southgate Center)
Massapequa Park
516-795-8330
If it's a cold day and you crave something hearty, then head over to this charming and popular trattoria for a bracing bowl of pasta. If it's lighter fare you desire, then the offshoot Cafe Butera, a few doors down, offers sandwiches, salads and soups. Prices are reasonable in both locations, and the service is unfailingly friendly.

Tai Show
4320 Merrick Rd.
Massapequa
516-798-3958
Slip your shoes off and retreat into one of the intimate tatami rooms at this hospitable Japanese restaurant where the sushi is ever-fresh and the cooked fare is light but sustaining. The midday menu offers some excellent bargains.

Mixing Bowl Eatery
2601 Merrick Rd.
Bellmore
516-826-7971
You'll find some wonderful American bistro specialties at this unpretentious contemporary cafe along Merrick Road. There are salads, sandwiches, as well as more substantial entrees — everything prepared with lots of flavor. Specials run the gamut from innovative to homey. You'll have to try hard to spend a lot.

PAUMANOK: A WRITER'S ISLAND

Long Island's fertile literary soil has nourished many a distinguished writer. It was in Great Neck that F. Scott Fitzgerald wrote "The Great Gatsby," while the French author Antoine de Saint Exupery penned "The Little Prince" at a house in Asharoken. Nearby, in Northport, Beat Generation Jack Kerouac spent some riotous days and nights, many of them at Gunther's bar. Sadly, today, little remains to see of the Long Island days of these authors. Happily, however, there are three writers — William Cullen Bryant, Christopher Morley and, of course, Walt Whitman — whose homes and workplaces have been restored, curated and opened to an appreciative public. Here, then, is a tour to inspire the muse in all of us.

Cedarmere

In a quaint and stately house the color of fog, the poet, newspaperman, civic leader and classical scholar William Cullen Bryant lived and worked for more than 30 years. As you climb up the hillside overlooking Roslyn Harbor, pause, as Bryant must have done, to gaze at the peaceful harbor, the tranquil pond and gardens. Bryant's works resonated with awe at the harmony between man and nature, a harmony one feels while walking paths and footbridges of his estate.

Built in 1787 by Richard Kirk, a Quaker, Cedarmere became Bryant's home from 1843, when he was 49, until his death in 1878, when he passed it on to family members. Although a fire destroyed

Newsday Photo / Bill Davis

Walt Whitman's birthplace and home in Huntington

parts of the house in 1902, many of the original sections remain intact.

Two rooms and a hallway have been restored to Bryant's time, about 1874. Surprisingly, the house had indoor plumbing. The woodwork in the parlor is painted the original celadon color, and the upholstered furniture also is from Bryant's day, as are the shelves which hold family keepsakes. Other pieces are antiques representative of the era. Much — but not all — of the artwork you'll see belonged to the Bryant family.

Artists, especially those associated with the Hudson River school of art, were frequent visitors to Cedarmere. In the house, you'll find a painting by Thomas Richardson as well as one by Frederick Kensett; there's also a reproduction of "Kindred Spirits," the famous Asher Durand work which depicts Bryant and the painter Thomas Cole as two tiny figures on a bluff high in the Catskill Mountains.

You'll find some interesting items when you visit the butler's pantry — family china, crystal and silver, as well as a bowl dedicated to Bryant from his grandchildren. These were among a cache of items formerly locked away in an old safe, which the museum's curator was able to pick open without knowing the combination.

On the second floor, you can view some of the other finds from that safe, among them, a wallet with crisply folded Civil War money, a lock of Bryant's hair, and Bryant's glasses. A diary, also unearthed, is now being transcribed.

Among the memorabilia on display upstairs is a rather odd photograph of Bryant in Turkish attire. The story goes that Bryant returned from an 1853 trip to Turkey both suntanned and bearded — so changed that his own staff didn't know who he was. In a rare display of humor, he put on a fez and Turkish robes and went to a neighbor's house, speaking in gibberish, unrecognized. It was an offbeat moment, immortalized by a friend who persuaded Bryant to allow his picture to be taken.

Outdoors, you can stroll through the magnificent landscaped gardens. Be sure to pick up a map that includes identifications of the exotic trees on the property, some planted by Bryant himself. And don't miss the quaint Gothic mill, built by Bryant in 1863; the top level functioned as a summer house, while the bottom was a working mill. Many believe that this is the oldest and probably the only surviving Gothic mill in the country.

The Knothole

It is, perhaps, the fantasy of every writer to have a cozy little retreat all to oneself, an adult version of a child's playhouse where one may think and write and not be bothered by the thousand distractions of the world outside.

Christopher Morley, an essayist, critic, and novelist best known for "Kitty Foyle," had such a hideaway on the property of his Roslyn home. Although that property has long since been sold, the little cabin, built in 1934 when he was 44, he called the Knothole was moved to its current site, within the Nassau County Park in Roslyn that bears his name, thanks to a group called the Christopher Morley Knothole Association. Go up the rustic path that leads from the parking lot to the cabin, and you'll enter another era entirely.

Over the doorway is a Latin inscription which, roughly translated, means "Working assiduously in the library is Paradise." The cottage is sparsely furnished; there are Morley's worktable, a built-in cot, some books, a rocking chair and lamp, in addition to a small display about Morley's life and contributions to American literature. But just outside the front door is a truly remarkable attraction: a futuristic "Dimaxion" bathroom, built in 1937 by Buckminster Fuller, a good friend of Morley's, who died in 1957. Picture an early version of an airplane rest room, complete with medicine chest, sink, shower and stall.

Walt Whitman Birthplace, State Historic Site And Visitors Interpretive Center

His head thrown back, his collar open, his demeanor jaunty, the Good Gray Poet, Walt Whitman, beckons us, more than a century after his death, to revel in the miracle of the everyday. His

Directions

To Cedarmere
Long Island Expressway to exit 39. Take Glen Cove Road to the third traffic light north of Northern Boulevard. Make left, going under railroad trestle. Turn left at stop sign, and then bear right onto Bryant Avenue. Take Bryant Avenue to the traffic light and bear left; the entrance to Cedarmere's parking lot is on your right, approximately four-tenths of a mile beyond the light. There is no access northbound on Bryant Avenue from Roslyn Village.

To The Knothole
Long Island Expressway to Searingtown Road, exit 36 north. Take Searingtown Road north one-half block; right into Christopher Morley Park. The Knothole is up path left of the parking lot.

To Walt Whitman Birthplace
Long Island Expressway to exit 49 north. Head north 1.8 miles, then make left onto Old Walt Whitman Road. Museum will be on right.

---

poetry sang of lust and human sexuality, of sweat, of beauty, of nature, of death, and of all that it means to be alive. It is said that when he sent a copy of "Leaves of Grass," a collection of his poems, to the poet John Greenleaf Whittier, Whittier read it, threw it in the fireplace, and burned it as obscene. Ralph Waldo Emerson, on the other hand, adored the collection of poems, which captured the cultural changes in America over a 35-year period.

Whitman's view of America truly started "from Paumanok," (the Indian name for Long Island), where, in 1819, he was born. Back then, West Hills was commonly known as Whitmanland, after the family that had settled there during the 17th Century.

Allow at least one hour to visit the birthplace and to spend time at the recently opened Visitors Interpretive Center and Library. Here, you'll view an 18-minute video retrospective of Whitman's life and career as a Long Island poet. This is where you'll see the only authentic Whitman piece of furniture that remains — the desk at which he wrote "Leaves of Grass." You'll want to spend lots of time studying the fascinating collection of more than 130 portraits of Whitman, who was anything but camera-shy, as well as a first edition of "Leaves of Grass," which he published in 1855, a schoolmaster's desk, and other artifacts, among them the original printing press of the Long Islander, a newspaper Whitman founded at 19.

You'll learn more about Whitman's history on your guided tour of the house his family left shortly before Walt's fourth birthday. Whitman spent the remainder of his childhood in Brooklyn, where the family grew and its finances diminished. He went to school until age 11, after which he worked as a printer's assistant and typesetter. At 16, Whitman returned to Long Island, where he worked as a schoolteacher in East Norwich, Hempstead, Babylon, Huntingt03 Station and Smithtown. He took off a year and a half to found the Long Islander before returning to teaching. But newspaper work was what he loved most, and over 18 years, Whitman was editor at several publications, among them the Long Island Star and the Brooklyn Eagle. During this period of his life, Whitman wrote and published the first edition of "Leaves of Grass."

In the Civil War, Whitman went to Fredricksburg, Va., where he searched for and found his battle-weary brother, George Washington Whitman. Moved by the sights he saw, he decided to stay on to work as a volunteer nurse. It is believed that an accidental slip of a surgeon's knife, which nicked his finger with gangrenous material, led to the ultimate decline of Whitman's health.

Following the war years, Whitman published a collection of poetry called "Drum Taps," whose second edition included the poem "When Lilacs Last in Dooryards Bloom'd," inspired by Lincoln's assassination. Following a stroke at age 65, Whitman lived with his brother, and, later, bought a house in Camden, N.J. He was never truly healthy and died there in 1892.

The house where Whitman's journey began was built by his father. The building incorporated a number of unusual features, such as wider doorways, higher ceilings, more window panes, built-in closets. Be sure to ask for the "find the feature" paper when you enter, which will help you to locate some of the more distinctive architectural attributes. You'll see accoutrements of everyday life — a whale-oil betty lamp, a press for soft fruits, some candlemaking equipment. The "borning room" where Whitman's mother gave birth to him also serving as a spare bedroom.

There are free maps for an auto-hiking tour of Whitman-related sites in West Hills, among them Whitman's beloved Jayne's Hill, the highest point on Long Island.

Important Information

Cedarmere
Bryant Avenue
Roslyn Harbor
516-571-8130

Open: Late April through early November; Saturdays and holidays, 10 a.m. to 4:45 p.m.; Sundays, 1 p.m. to 4:45 p.m.
Fee: Free
Tours: Self-guided
Rest rooms: Yes
On-site food: No
Wheelchair access: Yes (including a stairolator to the second floor)
Gift shop: Yes
Child appropriate: For older children

The Knothole
Christopher Morley Park
Searingtown Road
Roslyn
516-571-8113

Open: July to October, Sunday only, 1 p.m. to 4:45 p.m.
Fee: Free
Tours: No
Rest rooms: In park
On-site food: Concession in park
Wheelchair access: Yes
Gift shop: No
Child appropriate: Yes

Walt Whitman Birthplace, State Historic Site And Visitors Interpretive Center
246 Old Walt Whitman Rd.
Huntington Station
516-427-5240

Open: Memorial Day to Labor day, open daily 11

a.m. to 4 p.m.; the rest of the year, Wednesday to Friday, 1 p.m. to 4 p.m.; Saturday and Sunday, 11 a.m. to 4 p.m.; closed holidays.
Fee: $3 adults, $2 seniors 62 and over and students, $1 children 7 to 12, children under 6 free.
Tours: Yes
Rest rooms: In interpretive center
On-Site Food: Picnic facilities
Wheelchair access: Yes
Gift shop: Museum shop and bookstore
Child appropriate: Yes

Where to Eat

Chicken Shish Kebab
92 Mineola Ave.
Roslyn Heights
516-621-6828
You won't find much atmosphere at this little Greek and Mideastern luncheonette, but there are few places that serve a more succulent chicken souvlaki sandwich. Even the salads are fresher, brighter than the ordinary.

Pirandello
36 Lincoln Ave.
Roslyn Heights
516-625-6688
The mark of a noteworthy Italian restaurant just may be the quality of the marinara sauce, and the sauce served at Pirandello is a real winner. Garlic rolls — truly topnotch — come with a bowlful of that sauce, to dip at will. Pizza and pasta dishes, too, are lusty and flavorsome.

Jani
350 Rt. 110
Huntington Station
516-433-0622
After a day's touring, this serene Chinese-Japanese restaurant across the street from the Walt Whitman Birthplace provides welcome respite. Not only is the fare a cut above the commonplace, but they've also got wonderful Western-style desserts.

A SUNDAY AFTERNOON SOUTH SHORE SAMPLER

All you need for this small community-oriented tour is a free Sunday afternoon, a keen eye and an ear for a good story or two. You'll board a wonderful old railroad car, enter a Victorian parlor, visit a turn-of-the-century schoolroom and enjoy a host of memories.

Sunday is the one day all three of these places are open, and even though it might appear that there's only a two-hour span in which to do the tour, both the Wantagh and Seaford sites are willing to open early by appointment.

Wantagh Preservation Society And Museum

The observant traveler cruising southward on busy Wantagh Avenue may do a double-take when off in a little field on the right, a quaint Victorian station house and a very old railroad car come into view. This is the home of the Wantagh Preservation Society and Museum.

Inside the station house, you'll learn that the building dates to 1885, a time when Wantagh was known as Ridgewood (the name was changed in 1891, to avoid confusion with the Ridgewood in Queens). In 1966, when the railroad tracks along Sunrise Highway were elevated, the structure was moved to its current location. It has been carefully restored, right down to the old ticket cage; you can even view a photograph of the original ticket agent.

Newsday Photo / Daniel Goodrich

At the 1885 Wantagh railroad station, now a museum

In an exhibit entitled "Then and Now," the growth and change of Wantagh have been chronicled through snapshots of the old station, and before-and-after pictures of various sites in the community. Visitors can have fun comparing the old images with the current ones, and, later on, driving past those sites. Note, for example, that the building once occupied by Wantagh's original hook and ladder company is now home to an auto body shop with a distinctly Victorian roof.

You'll see other memorabilia, including a lovely stained glass window from the Wantagh Memorial Congregation Church, which was built in 1888 but razed in 1964. Another display relates to Jones Beach and includes a 1945 photograph of the Wantagh State Parkway.

Once you've seen the museum, step outside and climb the steep steps of the Jamaica, a deluxe 1912 parlor car still undergoing painstaking restoration to its former state of glory.

And what glory! Those of us who travel the railroad today know nothing of such luxury. Built expressly for the Long Island Rail Road and frequently used by its president in the early part of the century, the car carried well-heeled commuters out to Montauk. They willingly paid a premium in order to spend the long journey relaxing in truly homelike surroundings.

The first compartment resembles a parlor in a Victorian house, with fine woodwork, upholstered furniture, and amenities such as a pipe rack. Staterooms are furnished with beds as well as bathroom facilities; the largest compartment even has its own stall shower. Further back is the dining room and kitchen; the custom was to eat dinner on the way out to Montauk and breakfast on the way back. Note the special railroad china and silver used to set the graciously appointed table. It's hard to imagine that entire meals were prepared in the small galley and butler's pantry we see, but that, indeed, was the case. Ask your guide to tell you how the Wantagh Preservation Society came into possession of the Jamaica.

Seaford Historical Society

Old stuff. Lots of old stuff.
That's the initial impression you get when entering the cavernous building that houses the Seaford Historical Society's collections. And while there's some truth in this perception, there's meaning and order and a sense of a town's history awaiting discovery.

Even the building has a story to tell. Built in 1893-94, it was originally a schoolhouse facing out onto Jackson Avenue. In later years, it was moved to another site and became the Seaford Fire Department's headquarters, as well as a community hall. In 1975, the structure was offered to the Historical Society, which had it moved to its current foundation. It was on the auspicious date of July 4, 1976 — the nation's Bicentennial — that the Seaford Historical Society opened to the public.

Start your tour at the collection of parlor furniture, a mostly turn-of-the-century assortment of Empire and Victorian pieces donated by local families. You'll spot a cradle inscribed with the date 1644. It was given to the museum by the Johnson family, who resided in the historic Jackson House in Wantagh.

Then, there's a collection of carpentry and farming implements. Ask the museum attendant to tell you some of the stories about the two-man tree-saw, the ice-saw, the sauerkraut-maker — and you'll find yourself on a fascinating time-trip.

In another part of the room stands the Seaford Skiff, a shallow-bottomed bayman's duck-hunting boat made by Charles Verity of Bellmore in 1906. The Mystic Seaport Museum, which deemed it one of the best surviving examples of its genre, actually came to Seaford to copy the boat for its own collection.

Among other attractions, you'll find a

Directions

To Wantagh Preservation Society and Museum
Southern State Parkway to Wantagh Avenue south; Museum is about halfway between Jerusalem Avenue and Sunrise Highway; look for green sign on west side of street.

To Seaford Historical Society and Museum
Take Seaford Oyster Bay Expressway to end at Merrick Road, head east to Jackson Avenue, which is third traffic light from expressway; go one block north to corner of Waverly; make left, and quick left into parking lot.

To Lauder Museum
From Seaford Historical Society: Merrick Road to Route 110; left on Route 110; bear left at fork in the village museum is on the right.

---

wonderful array of community photographs. There's the 1914 diploma of Elsie Eldert, a young woman whose handwritten graduation address speaks eloquently of women's rights and the suffrage movement. Stop into small schoolroom, too, whose antique desks have seats and tops that fold away.

And more. If you have the time this place has the memories.

Amityville Historical Society: Lauder Museum

Housed in a turn-of-the-century brick and marble Greek Revival building is this charmingly offbeat museum filled with curios from Amityville's past.

Newsday Photo / Daniel Goodrich

The Lauder Museum, which has a variety of exhibits

While some exhibits are permanent, many change on a monthly and yearly basis.

You can always be sure of finding the ornate Victorian Parlor, with many furnishings donated by the locally prominent Strang family. Note the two Gothic organs, the antique typewriters, the high chair, and a purple set of funerary dishes, used only after a death in the family. Nosier sorts can pore over some of the Strangs' postmarked correspondences, which date back to 1902.

In another part of the museum, you'll see some of the pastoral works of artist Evangeline Worth Squires; her painting of cows drinking at Ireland Pond (now Avon Lake) recalls quite another Amityville from the one we know today. Huge photographs on the upper walls show a 1909 celebration inaugurating the trolley that ran from the Ocean Avenue village dock all the way up to Halesite. Look closely and, among the town dignitaries, you'll spot guest speaker Alfred E. Smith, the future governor.

Also on display are some interesting old carriages and sleighs. The Bellamy trap, used by the Stoddard family, features a back seat that drops down to reveal a concealed seat for the stable boy. An 1875 swell-bodied cutter, used by the Ireland family, looks as though it came from an old Currier and Ives print.

Then, there's the Bay Room, dedicated to the nautical life of the area. Ornithologists might be interested in the collection of indigenous stuffed birds.

Part of the museum is set up as an old schoolroom. Nearby is a display of old high school yearbook pictures; look carefully, and you'll see William Lauder, class of 1940. Lauder, for whom the museum is named, is its president as well as the individual who obtained the building as a donation from its previous occupant, a bank.

And in the rear, step into the old kitchen, equipped with an ice box and coal-burning stove. There's a heavy iron kettle, a cider press, as well as a collection of old cooking implements. Antique cans and boxes recall products that no longer exist. Remember Bab-O? Bohack supermarkets?

Important Information

Wantagh Preservation Society and Museum
1700 Wantagh Ave., opposite Emric Avenue
Wantagh
516-826-8687

Open: April through October, Wednesday and Sunday, 2 p.m. to 4 p.m.; November, December, and March, Sunday 2 p.m. to 4 p.m.; closed January and February; all other times by appointment
Fee: Free; donations accepted
Tours: Informal, only
Rest rooms: Yes
On-site food: No
Wheelchair access: Steps at station house; railroad car not accessible
Gift shop: No
Child appropriate: Older children

Seaford Historical Society and Museum
3890 Waverly Ave.
Seaford
516-826-1150

Open: May through October, Sunday, 2 p.m. to 4 p.m.; othertimes by appointment only
Fee: Free; donations accepted
Tours: Informal, only
Rest rooms: Yes
On-site food: No
Wheelchair access: No
Gift shop: Yes
Child appropriate: Older children

Lauder Museum

170 Broadway
Amityville
516-598-1486

Open: Sunday, Tuesday, Friday, 2 p.m. to 4 p.m., year-round; other times by appointment
Fee: Donations accepted
Tours: Informal only
Rest rooms: Yes
On-site food: No
Wheelchair access: Yes
Gift shop: Yes
Child appropriate: Older children

Where to Eat

Dominick's Park Avenue
3340 Wantagh Ave.
Wantagh
516-781-7070
This sleek Wantagh gathering place offers snazzy surroundings — check out the mural in the main dining room — as well as lively, Italian-accented cuisine. On Sundays, there's a buffet brunch offered between 10 a.m. and 3 p.m., but if you're not a fan of buffets, omelets are cooked-to-order, and you can always get something off the dinner menu.

Delfina
3082 Jerusalem Ave.
Seaford
516-221-4546
Old-fashioned in the best sense of the phrase, this Seaford ristorante opens at 4 p.m. for Sunday dinner, which should coincide perfectly with the end of your tour. The menu successfully balances the traditional with the innovative, so don't be surprised if a few Southwestern or Asian specials are listed alongside the Italian favorites. Prices are moderate, too.

Empire Szechuan Gourmet
4902 Merrick Rd.
Massapequa Park
516-541-3333
This branch of the successful Manhattan-based Empire chain offers both Japanese and Chinese specialties, as well as dim sum, which are made to order rather than offered on a rolling cart. The food is reliably good, and if not overly adventurous, invariably comforting.

WHEN QUEENS WAS YOUNG

It's hard to believe that the thriving industrial and residential metropolis we know as Queens was once bucolic farmland, but such was the case until about 100 years ago.

On this tour, we'll journey back to a time before Shea Stadium or La Guardia Airport could even have been imagined. We'll visit the home of a signer of the Constitution, see a 19th Century Gothic Revival church, and ramble about the city's only working historic farm.

King Manor

Rufus King was, above all, a man of principle. He served as a major during the Revolutionary War, helped write and sign the U.S. Constitution, was a member of the U.S. Senate and ran unsuccessfully for president as a Federalist in 1816. A staunch opponent of slavery, he fought eloquently against the Missouri Compromise as a senator.

Born in 1755, King began his career in Massachusetts and moved to New York in 1788. In an era when most men of wealth owned slaves, King paid a staff of servants to care for his country estate.

Today, we can visit that estate, which is nestled into a verdant 11-acre park amid the bustle of downtown Jamaica. King Manor is one of the oldest historic house-museums in the country, open to the public since 1900. Far from being stuffy, however, it is an eminently user-friendly attraction run by a high-spirited staff.

Visitors are first seated in the emerald-green parlor, dominated by a portrait of King (a reproduction of the Gilbert Stuart original). Here, you can view a brief video about King Manor, originally a working farm, where King lived with his wife, Mary, and their two sons, one of whom,

Photo courtesy of King Manor Museum

A sculpture of Rufus King at the King Manor Museum

John Alsop King, went on to become governor of New York from 1857 to 1859. The video, as well of the tour to follow, invites interaction on the part of the tourist. At King Manor, there are no ropes cordoning off sacred spaces; the public is welcome to browse respectfully.

The structure of King Manor, although completed in 1811, 16 years before King's death, dates back to the 1750s, when it was just a small farmhouse. It had already been enlarged somewhat when King moved in, about 1806, and, over the next few years, nearly doubled in size. Throughout the tour, your guide will point to remnants of the house's earlier stages.

Rooms are painted their original colors, based on paint analysis and archaeological work. Although many artifacts and furnishings are original to the house, not everything you see is a King family antique. In the parlor, for example, the carpet is a reproduction, albeit an accurate one.

But the 18th-Century English-made piano in that room is the genuine article. Note the chair-rails along the walls, as well as the casters on the furniture. It was essential that furniture be easily pushed to the edges of a room when the family entertained, so that people could dance.

The parlor is just one of the rooms in the house designated an interior landmark by virtue of the fact that most of its contents are original. Other such rooms are throughout the house.

Directions
(map on opposite page)

To King Manor Museum
Take the E, J, or Z subway to Jamaica Center; F or R subway to Parsons Boulevard or Long Island Rail Road to Jamaica Station. Driving from the east: Grand Central Parkway to 168th Street; take service road to Parsons Boulevard, turn left, continue to Jamaica Avenue, turn right — museum is one block on right. From the west, exit at Parsons Boulevard, turn right at light, continue to Jamaica Avenue, proceed as above.

To Grace Church
Two blocks east on Jamaica Avenue from King Manor.

To Queens County Farm Museum
E or F subway to Kew Gardens / Union Turnpike Station. Transfer to Q44A-Union Turnpike bus to Little Neck Parkway. Walk North three blocks to museum entrance. By car: Grand Central Parkway to exit 24 (Little Neck Parkway). Go south on Little Neck Parkway three blocks to museum entrance. Or take the Long Island Expressway to exit 32 (Little Neck Parkway); south on Little Neck Parkway to museum entrance.

The dining room, is a visual knockout with distinctive curved walls painted a vibrant gold, a striking black and white floor cloth beneath the stately dining room table, and red-swagged curtains at the windows. Try not to be startled by the life-sized plaster statue of King poring over a book in the library, lined with huge glass-walled shelves which King imported from England to store his collection of more than 5,000 books. Look closely at the walls; what appears to be rich wood paneling turns out to be a cleverly done trompe l'oeil painted surface.

Climb the stately staircase to the second floor, where many of the rooms, still undergoing restoration, are stocked with antiques. Down a couple of steps to the right is a servants' area. Pause, for a moment, to examine the room painted a bright pink; it's considered something of a mystery.

The room is paneled expensively and is larger than the other servants' rooms. Some postulate that it was home to Eve Bush, a young girl the Kings discovered one evening near a bush. Hence her name. Bush was taken into the King household; the theory is that she was more of a daughter than a servant. You can see her grave, not far from where the Kings are buried, in the cemetery of the nearby Grace Church.

If you get lucky — or if you book one of the

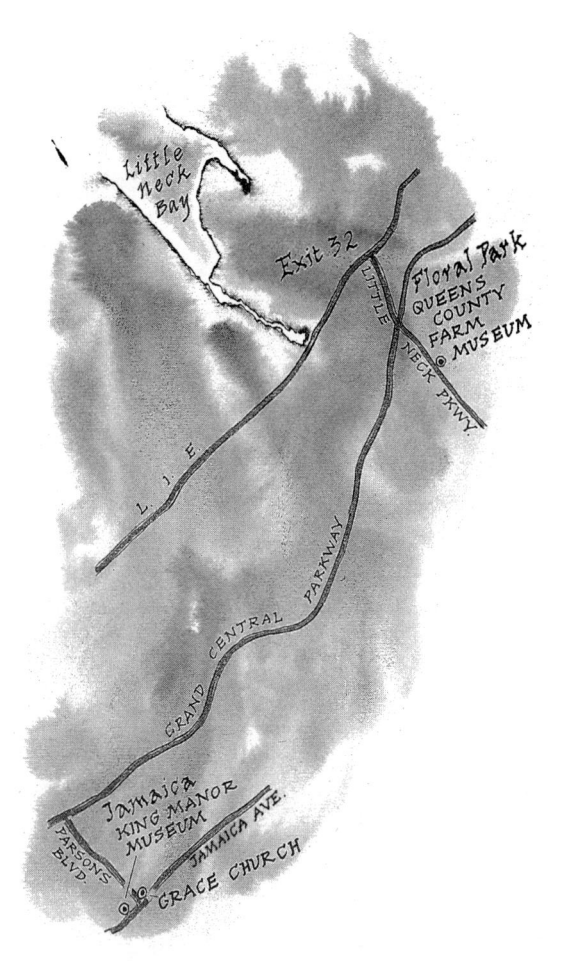

behind-the-scenes tours occasionally given — you might get to go up to the third floor, where the museum's caretaker, retired radio personality and historian, Roy Fox, lives. Among the interesting sights here are Fox' 4,000-book library and a storage room for the art work being curated.

Downstairs, again, you'll find yourself in the oldest part of the house. In the exhibit room that used to be the old parlor, there are some interesting interactive exhibits. You'll also see two kitchens, one from the 1750s, and a later, Victorian kitchen added by King's son.

Grace Church

After touring King Manor, walk two blocks east on Jamaica Avenue to Grace Episcopal Church. It is in the cemetery of this charming English Gothic

Two local inhabitants of the Queens County Farm Museum
Newsday Photo / Susan Farley

Revival church that the Kings and many of their descendants are buried.

Built during the 1860s, the structure you see is actually the third Grace Church to have been erected on this site. Its existence is partly because of the efforts of Gov. John Alsop King, in whose memory there is a beautiful interior bas-relief plaque. The 20th Century also is represented in a stunning WPA mural, done in 1933. Note the distinctive stained glass windows and the wood-ribbed vaulted ceilings.

Outside, in the cemetery, along with the weathered gravestones of Rufus and Mary King and their children, you'll also see the headstone of Eve Bush. Members of the prominent Gracie family, whose former mansion is now home to the mayor of of New York, are also buried in the churchyard.

Queens County Farm

Welcome to the only historical working farm in New York City, a place where children can meet barnyard friends, where families can go on hay rides (in season), and where anyone can purchase newly laid eggs. Wander among the outbuildings, built between the 1920s and 1930s; visit the apple orchard; go face-to-snout or -beak with pigs, geese, chickens, goats, cows and sheep.

On the premises is the Adriance farmhouse, which was built in 1772 and occupied by the family of the same name until 1833, when the Cox family bought and later expanded the house. Typically Dutch in design, its rooms are decorated to show the contrast between historic time periods.

The focal point of the 18th-Century kitchen, frequently the scene of Colonial cooking demonstrations, is the huge open hearth. An early 19th-Century kitchen has a more modern fireplace (with an arm for pots).

In the bedroom / parlor, there are original floors as well as a spinning wheel. The Cox family dining room, with its homey patterned wallpaper and plain muslin curtains, speaks of an era of comfortable simplicity, about the 1850s.

The Victorian parlor, however, tells another story. The ornate tin ceiling, red velvet chairs, and heavy curtains, give testimony to new money, which the Cox family acquired through trucking produce into the city and selling it.

This new-found affluence, coupled with the availability of manufactured goods, meant forsaking the homespun in favor of the store-bought. The era of conspicuous consumption had begun.

Important Information

King Manor Museum
King Park
Jamaica Avenue (between 150th and 153rd Streets)
Jamaica
718-206-0545

Open: March to December, Saturday and Sunday, noon to 4 p.m. (last tour 3:30 p.m.), second and last Tuesday of each month, 12:15 p.m. to 2 p.m.; call for special events; school and group tours by appointment.
Fee: $2 adults, $1 children
Tours: Yes.
Rest rooms: Yes
On-site food: No
Wheelchair access: Partial (entire first floor)
Gift shop: No
Child appropriate: Yes

Grace Church
155-24 90th (Rufus King) Ave.
Jamaica
718-291-4901

Open: Cemetery open at all times; church services noon daily, 8 a.m. Sunday. All other times, call for appointment.
Fee: Free
Tours: No
Rest rooms: No
On-site food: No
Wheelchair access: No
Gift shop: No
Child appropriate: Older children

Queens County Farm Museum
73-50 Little Neck Pkwy.
Floral Park
718-347-FARM (718-347-3276)

Open: Monday to Friday, grounds only, 9 a.m. to 5 p.m., free admission; Saturday and Sunday, grounds and tour of farmhouse, hay rides (weather permitting).
Fee: Free, except for special events
Tours: Farmhouse only
Rest rooms: Yes
On-site food: Picnic tables on site; cafe under construction
Wheelchair access: Yes
Gift shop: Yes
Child appropriate: Yes

Where to Eat

Maria Lucia
256-11 Union Tpke.
Glen Oaks
718-343-5458
In this unassuming little pizzeria-trattoria, you'll find superb calamari as well as some dynamite pizzas (the Grandma pie is a knockout). Pasta dishes, redolent of fresh garlic, are inexpensive.

Fratelli Iavarone Cafe
1534 Union Tpke. (Lake Success Center)
New Hyde Park
516-488-4500
Just over the Nassau County border is this superb little cafe, an offshoot of the Iavarone Brothers Gourmet Market. Pasta dishes and salads are fresh, original, stylishly presented and utterly delicious. The pizzas are standouts, too. Service is unfalteringly friendly, prices reasonable.

Tenjin
254-02 Northern Blvd.
Little Neck
718-279-1116
The sushi rolls are imaginative and fresh at this gracious Little Neck Japanese restaurant. Cooked fare rates highly, too. The special luncheon menu, Tuesday through Friday only, makes for a bargain-priced way to eat both healthfully and well.

HUNTINGTON'S HERITAGE

The Huntington area, thought of by many as the cultural hub of Long Island, is a history-buff's playground. We've selected three sites to visit, two in Huntington village itself, the third in nearby Centerport. Combine this tour with a stroll through the shopping district and a leisurely lunch or dinner, and you should have a full and satisfying outing.

David Conklin Farm House

When newlyweds David and Sybil Conklin, one of the early farming families in the community, moved in back in 1765, their house was just a modest three-room dwelling. It was here that the Conklins raised eight children; the ninth was born six months after David Conklin passed away.

No one is exactly certain how he died. Years earlier, David Conklin had been a prisoner during the Revolutionary War. Whether the toll that those years had taken on his health contributed to his death is unclear. Conklin did compose his will on Dec. 3, 1786, the day he died at age 42. Sybil Conklin died about a year later. Following her death, the house came into posession of David's cousin, Abel Conklin, who moved in with his wife, Ruth, and their four children. The presumption is that Abel and Ruth raised David and Sybil's younger children.

You realize, while touring the older section of the Conklin House, how fragile life was in those days. A sampler, made by a child at the Huntington Academy during the early part of the 19th Century, mourns the death of siblings. Look closely, and you'll see that the words "brother" and "sister" have been made plural by the later addition of the letter "s".

In the pantry-like keeping room, you'll see one of the only two Conklin pieces in the house — a field bed, an early forerunner of the Murphy bed. Years earlier, it had been found, tied up, among the beams

Newsday Photo / Patrick Andrade

Fragments of a stoneware jug, circa 1827, found beneath the Suydam House.

of the basement. Period pieces, like the drop-leaf tables, are indicative of the kind of furniture that was easily moved from the center of a room to make room for other activities.

Since Huntington was on the edge of what was then Queens County, the predominantly English decor included some Dutch elements, as evidenced by the large kas or wardrobe. A lap-loom, used for weaving, dates to the 1600s. You'll also see a chair where George Washington is said to have sat when he visited Platt's Tavern in Huntington in 1790. There's also a table, reputed to have been used by Washington when he stopped at Ketcham's Tavern in Amityville.

In the kitchen, near the hearth, you can check out the early, rudimentary versions of a toaster, a waffle iron and a reflecting oven. You'll also see a few pieces of pottery from the then-renowned Huntington pottery works; others are showcased in an exhibit room you'll view at the end of your tour. A huge oven used to bake bread for the British troops was discovered underneath the stairwell leading to the basement. Chits were unearthed, stating that the British owed Mrs. Conklin money for bread.

The center hall was part of an extension added onto the house during the Federal Period, between 1820 and 1840. Here, you'll see the more formal and traditional front parlor used for entertaining and a unique box piano, reputed to be the first of its kind on Long Island. In the back part of room, which was added on to the house during the Victorian period, you'll also see specimens of taxidermy, so popular with the men of the era; hence, the birds under glass. Take note of the small chest between the windows; it's the second of the original Conklin pieces in the house.

After viewing the rooms, give a parting thought to the last Miss Conklin, who took in boarders for a living. When she died in 1912, she willed the house to the Huntington Historical Society.

Dr. Daniel Kissam House

Kissam is the K. in millionaire William K. Vanderbilt's name. But, the Kissam family goes further back in America's past than the more famous Vanderbilt clan as you'll learn when you visit the home of Daniel Kissam, a country doctor.

Kissam, like all medical practitioners of his day, made house calls. In 1795, he moved his thriving medical practice from Oyster Bay to Huntington, where he had this home built by the prominent housewright Timothy Jarvis. After Kissam suffered a stroke in 1830, his son-in-law, Charles Sturges, also a doctor, took over the practice. Kissam, however, continued to live in the house until his death in 1839.

You enter through the center hall into the front parlor. Note the floor cloth, which has been reproduced by copying a little bit of the original, fortuitously found by museum volunteers.

The formal dining room, which Kissam remodeled out of the original kitchen, must have been a stately place to dine. This floor cloth was original to the expanded 1840 house. In wintertime, servants would take it up, beat it, clean it and then sew it back down again.

The back parlor is painted the original barn red; you can see the old floorboards, which were uncovered in 1983. Currently, the kitchen wing is under restoration, but your tour guide will fill you in on the many incarnations the kitchen has had.

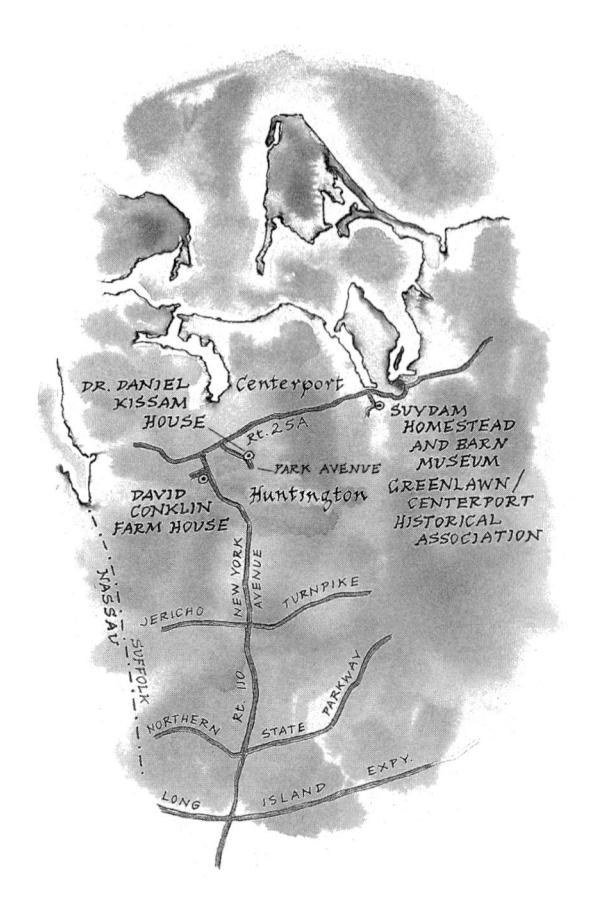

Directions

To David Conklin Farm House
Northern State Parkway or Long Island Expressway to Route 110 and go north. Route 110 becomes New York Avenue after crossing Jericho Turnpike. Continue about two miles; the Conklin House is at the corner of High Street and New York Avenue.

To Dr. Daniel Kissam House
From Conklin House: Continue north on New York Avenue to Main Street (Route 25A); make right and proceed to Park Avenue, where you will turn right. House is about one-eighth of a mile on left.

To Suydam Homestead and Barn Museum (Greenlawn/Centerport Historical Association)
From Kissam House: Take Park Avenue north to Route 25A and head east about two miles. Turn right at Centerport Road; parking lot to museum is on left.

When you go upstairs, you'll pass a Seth Thomas clock, donated to the museum by the Wood family of Huntington. Ask about the connection between this and the original Kissam piece, which you'll find at the top of the stairs.

Upstairs, there's a room devoted to the Kissam family tree and its roots in America. Daniel Kissam, you'll see, first married Elizabeth Tredwell, with whom he had seven children. After her death, he married Phebe Oakley, who bore him another seven.

And then, of course, there's the famed Vanderbilt connection. Interestingly, when a relative, Maria Louise Kissam, married William Henry Vanderbilt, father of William K., in 1840, it was the Kissam family that was considered "high society."

In another upstairs room, whose woodwork is painted and glazed a distinctive olive green, you'll see more period pieces, among them a spinning wheel and some early chairs. A child's room showcases an amazingly realistic rocking horse carved of wood and covered with real horse's hair. And you'll also find some quaint child-sized furniture. On your way out, stop into the gift shop, which is really a consignment market for local antiques.

Suydam Homestead and Barn Museum

In 1992, while removing floorboards from the west wing of the Suydam house in Centerport, museum volunteers came across a cache of broken pottery and china. An archaeologist was called in, and by the summer of 1993, a remarkable collection of 18th and 19th Century redware and china had been unearthed.

Today, you may see this pottery at a fascinating exhibit housed in the Suydam Homestead and Barn. Built about 1730 and occupied by members of the Suydam family from the late 18th Century to 1957, the house is a gateway to other times, its various rooms a patchwork of the previous two centuries.

Through the entry vestibule, one can easily see where the old house begins. Although the shingles on the back of the house are replacements, those in the front are original. Your guide will explain the history of each of the rooms, one of which was connected to the main house in later years. Note the huge chimney, which is shared by three fireplaces, the one in the kitchen containing a beehive oven, so named for its shape.

The main attraction, though, is the West Wing, where the pottery and china are on display. The redware was manufactured in Huntington, which was at one time a great center for potters, some of whom came from Connecticut. There's also pearlware, creamware and some Staffordshire pieces imported from England. You can view a collection of other archaeological finds from the property, among them Indian pottery, spearheads, old musket balls, the bones of a dog and skeleton of a loon's head.

In the nearby barn, you'll see agricultural memorabilia from local families. There are two farm wagons and a cutter, along with a variety of farm implements. Coopers' tools as well as a Rothman's Pickle sign, are leftovers from the era of the Greenlawn pickle works, which flourished from the 1890s through the 1920s. A poignant note is the memorial stone for Reuben Suydam, son of Cornelius and Phoebe Suydam, who died September, 1852. It was discovered recently by a group of Eagle scouts working on a project on the property.

Upstairs, you'll find a collection of Suydam furniture that includes a beautiful sleigh bed. The oldest coverlet in the collection, which dates from 1824, has the name of Phoebe Remph woven into it.

Important Information

David Conklin Farm House
2 High St.
Huntington
516-427-7045

Open: Tuesday to Friday and Sunday, 1 p.m. to 4 p.m.; closed Saturday
Fee: $2.50 for adults, $1 children under 12, $5 family (not including grandparents)
Tours Yes
Rest rooms: Yes, but very basic
On-site food: No
Wheelchair access: No
Gift shop: At Kissam House only
Child appropriate: Older children

Dr. Daniel Kissam House
434 Park Ave.
Huntington
516-427-7045

Open: May to October, Sunday, 1 p.m. to 4 p.m. or by appointment
Fee: $2.50 for adults, $1 children under 12, $5 family (not including grandparents)
Tours: Yes
Rest rooms: Yes
On-site food: No
Wheelchair accessible: first floor only
Gift shop: Yes

Child appropriate: Older children

Suydam Homestead and Barn Museum (Greenlawn-Centerport Historical Association)
1 Ft. Salonga Rd. (Route 25A)
Centerport
516-754-1180

Open: June through October, Sundays, 1 p.m. to 4 p.m..
Fee: Free
Tours: Yes
Rest rooms: No
On-site food: No
Wheelchair access: Partial
Gift shop: Yes
Child appropriate: Older children

Where to Eat

Abel Conklin's
54 New St.
Huntington
516-385-1919
Built in the early half of the 19th Century, this restaurant was once home to Abel K. Conklin, a town official and descendant of the Abel Conklin who first inherited the David Conklin home. The place has a warm, clubby decor and offers a simple steak house menu, along with salads, burgers, and sandwiches. The food is both satisfying and moderately priced.

Bali
23 Wall St.
Huntington
516-271-8487
In the mood for something a bit exotic? Try the creative, tropical-themed cuisine at this unusual eatery. At lunch, you'll find, in addition to some exciting entrees, a roster of imaginative sandwiches and salads. Dinner is quite well-priced, considering the presentation and caliber of the fare.

Ahrash Restaurant
256 Main St.
Huntington
516-351-2149
Open for dinner only, this Middle Eastern-Turkish hideaway in the heart of Huntington offers fare as exotic as it is satisfying. After a full day's touring, you might find this just the place to unwind.

HEMPSTEAD AND GARDEN CITY

The contrast of the old and the new is probably nowhere more graphic than in Hempstead, settled during the 1600s just south of the vast Hempstead Plains. Today, in the shadow of a huge concrete multilevel parking facility in Hempstead, you'll find a serene white Colonial church surrounded by a graveyard dotted with crumbling tombstones. A few blocks away is a little gem of a museum devoted to the African-American experience. Conclude your tour in Garden City at the magnificent neo-Gothic Cathedral of the Incarnation, where you'll learn about the roots of a planned community as well as the romantic story of the cathedral built in memory of the town's founder.

St. George's Episcopal Church

As incongruous as St. George's Church appears amid the bustle of modern Hempstead, this Colonial landmark also is a reassuring reminder of a past still connected to the world of today. On a weekday, and you'll see children on their way to nursery school in the modern connected building; on a weekend, the sanctuary is filled with worshipers.

The church was first born as a meetinghouse in 1648, five years after Hempstead was first settled. It was replaced by a second, larger meetinghouse in 1673, before the church itself was established in 1702 by ordained missionaries from England. The church still owns the silver chalice, paten and prayer book sent by Queen Anne of England, on a ship that was captured by pirates, who used the chalice as

Newsday Photo / K. Wiles Stabile

The Cathedral of the Incarnation in Garden City

an eating vessel. But the booty was recovered, and, by 1710, had finally reached the church.

It wasn't until 1735 that the first real church building for St. George's was erected, replacing the old meetinghouse. The church's golden cock weathervane still shows the impressions made by musket balls during the Revolutionary War by soldiers at target practice. Parts of that church were incorporated into the building that stands today, which was built in 1822.

Today's church's altar is believed to be the original one, although research on that continues. When the building was constructed, the pillars were fashioned of oak hewn from Hempstead Plain. The church's sanctuary was remodeled in 1906, a renovation paid for by financier August Belmont, whose family pew is marked by a plaque.

You cannot help but notice the beauty of the

church's stained glass windows. Although they're not Tiffany originals, several were fashioned after Tiffany designs. One window depicts the religiously symbolic legend of St. George and the dragon.

After viewing the sanctuary, step outside and look across the street to the Rectory, which has been in continuous use since 1793. Then look up at the clock on the church's tower, made in 1854 by the firm of Sherry and Bryan of Sag Harbor.

A walk through the graveyard is a tour through history. Samuel Seabury, a rector at St. George's and the father of the first Episcopal bishop in the United States, is buried here, along with members of his family. You'll also find the headstones of several Revolutionary War soldiers from prominent Long Island families, among them Samuel Carman and Joseph Cheesman. The oldest identifiable stone, however — a Puritan gravestone dated 1725 — was stolen during the late 1970s, shortly after its photograph appeared with a newspaper article.

African American Museum

Small only in size, the African American Museum in Hempstead lives by its mission statement: "to preserve, collect, restore, and disseminate information about African-American history and culture on Long Island." Anyone who looks insightfully at its collection of paintings, sculpture and artifacts will find it difficult not to be moved by the rich and complex heritage embodied therein.

While exhibitions change periodically, there's usually a basic core of works on permanent display. You'll see Lawrence artist Raymond Wallace's colorful and symbolic painting which depicts the Rev. Martin Luther King Jr. in front of of two families, one black and impoverished, the other white and affluent. Another Wallace work deals candidly with the issue of bus segregation in the South. A multidimensional painting done on barnboard by artist Robert Carter shows an African-American mother and her children, illustrating simultaneously the plight of the single mother as well as the inherent holiness of the mother-child relationship.

Throughout the museum, you'll also see sculptures by James Counts, a local artist and active supporter of the museum. A bust of a black soldier, entitled "Many Thousand Gone," tells the story of those who died in defense of a sometimes ungrateful nation. Another Counts bust, this one of Underground Railroad founder Harriet Tubman, shows a noble face weathered by years of hardship.

In a more lighthearted vein, Maxine Townsend-

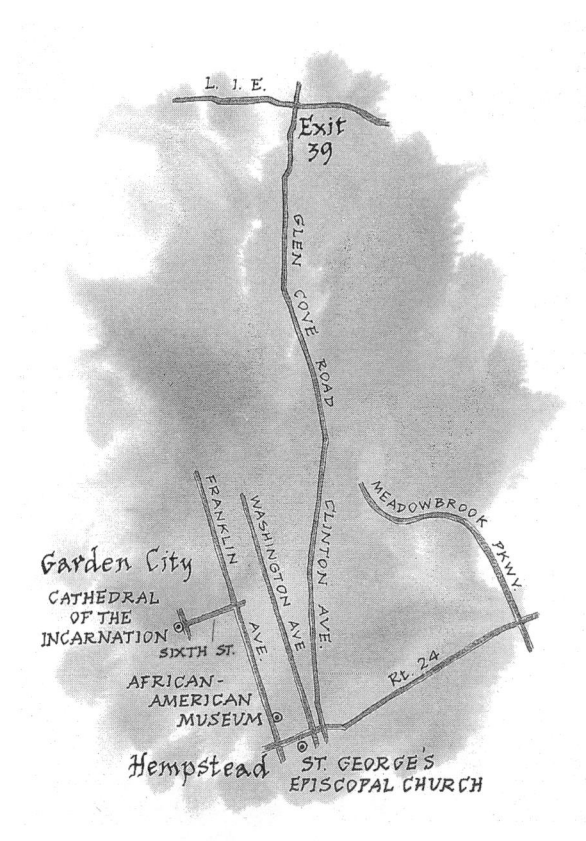

Directions

To St. George's Episcopal Church
Long Island Expressway to exit 39 south. Take Glen Cove Road through Garden City (it becomes Clinton Avenue) into Hempstead. Half a block after Route 24, make a right before firehouse. Cross Washington Street, go to multi-level parking on left. Park on far left side; church is opposite north wall of parking lot, accessible through opening in concrete wall.

To African American Museum
Meadowbrook Parkway to Route 24 west, which becomes Fulton Street; turn right onto Franklin Avenue; museum is on right.

To Cathedral of the Incarnation
Continue north on Franklin Avenue to Sixth. Left on Sixth, continue past railroad station, crossing Hilton and Cathedral; make a left approximately 10 feet after Cathedral Avenue, into drive. Parallel-park on any of the drives around the Cathedral.

Broderick's "News Day at the River" tells of gossip along the river banks of a Caribbean land. And Huntington artist Jackie Cully's watercolor entitled "Katana" lovingly depicts a baby on a rug. There also are some traditional African garments, such as an early 20th-Century Nigerian robe, some lovely woven fabrics from Niger and a graceful curved turn-of-the-century stool from Ghana.

In another room, most often used for changing exhibits, music buffs can see jazz great Eubie Blake's piano, donated to the museum by his family.

Cathedral of the Incarnation

Call it a love story written in marble, iron and stained glass. So great was the adoration of Cornelia Stewart for her late husband, Alexander, that, shortly after his death in 1876, she commissioned a cathedral to be built in his memory. Alexander Stewart was, in fact, no ordinary citizen.

As the founding father of Garden City, Stewart had purchased the land for the village in 1869 at $55 an acre, carefully planning every aspect of its layout. He even had the Garden City Hotel and a special line of the Long Island Rail Road built to service the new, planned community for well-to-do citizens. Perhaps it is only fitting that the Gothic-style cathedral built in his memory remains, to this day, the showpiece of Garden City, its spires soaring high above the surrounding flatlands.

Yet the cathedral is somewhat less grand than originally envisioned by architect Henry S. Harrison of New York City. This is because Cornelia Stewart's attorney and financial adviser, Judge Henry Hilton, took it upon himself to cut costs by drawing lines through the blueprint, slicing off entire sections. When you enter the cathedral, look down at the floor's mosaic design, and you'll see a pattern that ends abruptly as though it has been cut cleanly in half.

The stained glass windows of the cathedral, designed by the English firm of Clayton and Bell, are particularly beautiful; follow them around the building, and you'll find the illustrated story of Jesus.

Biblical scholars who look closely will observe that the fourth and fifth windows are in reverse order; even cathedral-builders make mistakes. Note that the large transept windows are not part of the series; the North transept, known as the "Jesse Window," depicts Christ's earthly ancestors who were descended from the sleeping figure of Jesse; the South transept, called the "Te Deum" window, symbolizes major events in the life of Christ.

The cathedral is also the Seat of the Bishop of Long Island. And the organ is one of the Island's largest. Look closely at the baptistry, characterized by water symbols; at the base of the font, you'll see a charming little frog. Although the pillars of this cathedral might look as though they're made of stone, they're actually fashioned of iron. If you study the faces carved into the decorative elements of the church, you might find that of the architect himself. It's also interesting to note that all the flora and fauna in the carvings are native to Long Island.

The undercroft of the church showcases portraits of the various bishops who have served here. In a large glass case, you'll find the jewels, miter and coat of a previous bishop, James de Wolfe. The first flag of the Episcopal Church in America is also on display.

In the small and lovely Chapel of the Resurrection, both Alexander and Cornelia Stewart are believed to be buried in a crypt beneath the chancel. There is some doubt about Alexander Stewart, because, before the cathedral was completed, his body was stolen. Ultimately, a body was recovered, but, since nobody is certain that it was Stewart's, his presence in the crypt is mostly a matter of faith.

Important Information

St. George's Episcopal Church
319 Front St.
Hempstead
516-483-2771

Open: Call before coming; Monday to Friday, 9 a.m. to 2 p.m.; Saturday, 9 a.m. to noon.
Fee: Free
Tours: Informal
Rest rooms: Yes
On-site food: No
Wheelchair access: Yes
Gift shop: No
Child appropriate: older children

African American Museum
110 N. Franklin St.
Hempstead
516-572-0730

Open: Wednesday, 6 p.m. to 9 p.m.; Thursday to Saturday, 10 a.m. to 4:45 p.m.; Sunday, 1 p.m. to 4:45 p.m.
Fee: Donations accepted
Tours: Group tours only; call for details
Rest rooms: Yes

On-site food: No
Wheelchair access: Yes
Gift shop: Yes
Child appropriate: Yes

Cathedral of the Incarnation
50 Cathedral Ave.
Garden City
516-746-2955

Open: By appointment
Fee: Free
Tours: Informal and by appointment
Rest rooms: Yes
On-site food: No
Wheelchair access: Main floor only; no access to rest rooms
Gift Shop: No
Child appropriate: Older children

Where to Eat

Nakisaki
276 Fulton Ave.
Hempstead
516-292-9200
The showplace of Hempstead, this polished Jamaican-Chinese restaurant offers reasonably priced fare that's both spicy and unique. You'll have to look long and hard to find better jerk pork than Nakisaki's. You might want to opt for the a la carte menu rather than the serve-yourself buffet for lunch.

660 West
660 Franklin Ave.
Garden City
516-742-4745
This pub-style Garden City eatery, has a menu that goes from basic salads and burgers to more innovative wraps and entrees. Prices are moderate and service, is ever-friendly. Splurge on the calories for dessert.

Houston's
Roosevelt Field
Garden City
873-1454
In a dramatic, Art Deco-inspired setting, this handsome restaurant attached to Roosevelt Field offers some surprisingly fine fare. The Southwestern-inspired grilled chicken or the Asian-style seared tuna salad are two top choices.

NORTH SHORE NASSAU COUNTY

Away from the commerce and commotion of contemporary life, you can still find glimmers of yesterday on Nassau County's North Shore. On this tour, we'll visit prehistoric Long Island, colonial and Victorian Port Washington and the more contemporary global history of U.S. Merchant Marines. Expect a few surprises and count on spending the better part of a day, especially in fine weather.

Garvies Point Museum & Preserve

It's easy to forget that before Europeans crossed the ocean to colonize the New World, there was a Long Island. At the Garvies Point Museum & Preserve, you can get to know that Island during its prehistoric days.

And you'll learn about the American Indian inhabitants, viewing fragments from a rich culture all but destroyed.

Afterwards, you can walk on five miles of surrounding trails, encountering flora and fauna from woodland, meadow, and shoreline.

In the main room of the museum, you'll come, first, to an alcove dealing with the glaciers and formation of Long Island from the late cretaceous period until about 20,000 years ago.

Another alcove depicts the early Indian life on Long Island featuring beautiful figures made of clay and wax. In a showcase nearby, you'll see an Indian man fully arrayed for a spring ceremony in his deerskin cloak and deer claw necklace; in contrast, a woman wears traditional working dress, which, back then, meant only a skirt.

Here, too, you'll find a wonderful collection of

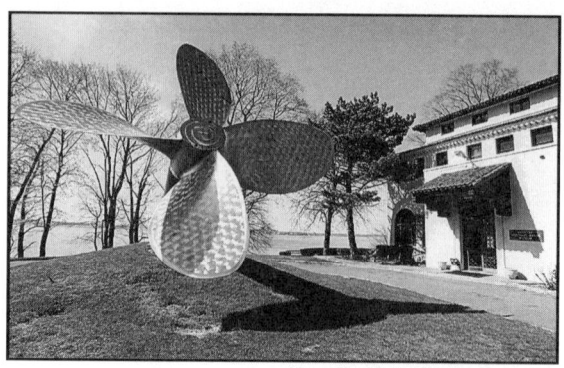

A troop ship propeller at the Merchant Marine Academy
Newsday Photo / Kathy Kmonicek

masks. Walk over to an exhibit on American Indian village life. Push a button, and an animatronic figure illustrates the knapping process by which two rocks are hit together to create a tool.

Another button activates the figure of a woman grinding corn. In a nearby alcove, you'll see a more somber exhibit, chronicling the death of the American Indian culture. Aspiring archaeologists will be fascinated with the enormous glass box in the center of the room, which graphically illustrates the process of a dig. There's also an interactive display featuring a replica of a human skeleton and, in another case, actual human bones, whose configurations demonstrate differences in sex and age.

Don't miss the rear porch, where, in addition to some old Indian artifacts, you'll find a replica of a dugout canoe, made from the wood of the tulip tree, and a model of a wigwam built by a contemporary Cree Indian. Outside, on one of the walking trails, you can see the Indian sweat lodge that he also built.

No visit to Garvies Point is complete without a look at the dinosaur footprint — the first and only such specimen found on Long Island. Fossil fanatics will love this place. Outdoor types can spend hours walking any number of trails, some of which lead down to the waterside. En route, you might see a woodpecker, an osprey, or even — if you get especially lucky — a fox.

Sands-Willets House

A visit to the Sands-Willets House is a walk through three centuries of Long Island life. While all the furnishings inside may not be original to the house itself, they have all been donated by local families and serve to remind visitors of the area's bygone days.

It helps to think of this three-section structure as

a sandwich; the first and oldest section was built in 1735 by John Sands III; the center hall as well as two upstairs rooms were added on around 1840, by Edmund Willets, a Quaker who had just purchased the house. In 1848, he added the Greek Revival east wing.

Enter the house in the middle of the sandwich, the lovely Federalist front hallway. To the right is a parlor decorated to represent the late Empire period, roughly 1860-1880. Of particular note is the breakfront, which comes from the nearby estate of renowned composer John Philip Sousa, whose grandfather, a cabinetmaker, built it. There's also an enchanting German music box, a fine old harpsichord, and a noteworthy collection of early American glass. In the adjacent room, you'll meet the Willets family, or at least their daguerreotype likenesses, which hang on the wall. The centerpiece of this room is the imposing concert grand piano, circa 1878. There's also a sewing table with a cunning little thimble box and two magnificent period costumes. Ask your guide to tell you the story of the letter, dated 1839, that was found in a secret compartment of the 1800 Irish writing desk.

At the top of the staircase, you'll find a mailbox whose inscription reads J.P. Sousa. Yes, this was, indeed John Philip's mailbox. His band uniform and traveling trunk are displayed alongside.

In the Victorian bedroom, along with toys, you'll find a man's shaving stand, a wedding fan, and some more period costumes. Somewhat out-of-period, but charming nonetheless, is a 1930's tennis outfit.

Before descending the staircase, ask your guide to give you a little demonstration of the pump organ in the hall.

Downstairs again, you'll visit the room currently used to display documents relating to the house's occupants. There's a picture of Willets as a younger man, a passport signed by Secretary of State William Seward, the man responsible for the purchase of Alaska, and an original poster from the Ford Theater advertising the very performance at which Lincoln was shot. Other documents relate to the pasturing of local cows.

The formal dining room boasts a beautiful Waterford chandelier, circa 1830, as well as Chamberlain Worcester china.

Passing through the exhibit room, whose displays change regularly, you'll enter the old section of the house, which dates back to around 1735. Here, where schoolchildren often come to do Colonial-style cookery, you'll see a hearth and Dutch oven. The beehive oven, formerly bricked over, was unearthed in 1971 and restored to its original appearance.
Behind that is the out-kitchen, where heavy work was done. Note the accoutrements of daily life - the

Directions

To Garvies Point Museum & Preserve
Long Island Expressway to exit 39 north (Glen Cove Road). Continue north past Northern Boulevard on Glen Cove by-pass (keeping left at fork) to last traffic light facing Glen Cove Fire House, turn right onto Brewster Street, go right, continuing to Cottage Row, where you make a left. Stay on Cottage Row, which becomes Landing Lane, following signs to the museum. You will make a left on to Germaine Street, a right onto McLoughlin Street, and a left onto Barry Drive, proceeding to park entrance.

To American Merchant Marine Museum at the U.S. Merchant Marine Academy
Long Island Expressway to exit 33, Community Drive. Follow Community Drive, East Shore Road, Hicks Lane (road changes names) to Middle Neck Road. Right onto Middle Neck Road to Steamboat Road (first light). Turn left and continue to Academy.

To Sands-Willets House (Cow Neck Peninsula Historical Society)
Long Island Expressway to exit 36 north (Searingtown Road); go north on Searingtown Road for 2.9 miles; (Searington becomes Port Washington Boulevard) house No. 336 on left. From Merchant Marine Academy, take Steamboat Road to Middle Neck Road; turn right and proceed to Northern Boulevard, where you turn left. Continue on Northern Boulevard to Searingtown Road (corner of Americana Shopping Center), where you turn left. Proceed as above.

toaster, the waffle iron, the cauldron, apple corer, candle molds, and enormous heavy duty egg beater. There's also a closet which, if opened, reveals a tiny, shallow staircase to the second floor. It looks difficult to negotiate, cramped and narrow. Think of it as a reminder of a time when comfort took a back seat to survival.

American Merchant Marine Museum

Housed in the Italian Renaissance mansion of inventor William S. Barstow, this museum on the property of the U.S. Merchant Marine Academy in Kings Point, rates as a gem. It will surprise and delight with its fine art, architecture and grand water view. And while, yes, you'll be seeing a lot of model ships, you'll also be learning about the bravery and spirit of those who dedicated their lives to a branch of service often overlooked by the general public. Outside the museum, looking like an enormous gold sculpture, is a 19-ton propeller taken from a World War P-2 troop ship. Once inside, you'll be amazed by the magnificent ceilings and woodwork in every hallway, vestibule and gallery.

To the right of the entryway is a gallery commemorating the Merchant Marine's role in World War II, which was to transport troops and materials for the other branches of the armed services. In the room, you'll see oil paintings such as the one commemorating the heroism of Midshipman Edwin O'Hara, killed aboard ship while holding off enemy fire. There are beautifully wrought models of ships, troop transports, and passenger vessels. Also on display is one of the five surrender swords presented by Japan to Gen. Douglas McArthur at the end of World War II. Stolen from the academy in 1971, it was returned, anonymously, in 1991 by an envoy of the dying, remorseful thief.

In the center hall, you'll find "Sparks," a lifesize model of a radio operator enclosed in a glass radio shack. An audio box outside the shack relates his story, complete with 1940's music. There are a total of 10 audio boxes in the museum, rendering the exhibits understandable to children as well as adults.

In the room known simply as Gallery 1, you'll have a chance to admire the stunning Waterford crystal chandelier as well as the commanding water view. Here, too, you also can see the wheel from the U.S.S. Constitution.

Perhaps the most emotionally powerful experience in the museum is the room dedicated to the 142 who died as students in active duty during

World War II. Their pictures — the pictures of young boys whose faces look eager to embark on life's adventures — line the walls. An audio box helps bring their story to life.

The Gallant Ship Gallery, which memorializes acts of valor of Merchant Marine ships, has as its centerpiece the huge 18-foot model of the S. S. Washington. Next door is a little gallery whose glass shelves are lined with teacups and saucers. These were collected by two Academy graduates who, as pilots on the Panama Canal, asked every ship passing through for one cup and one saucer. What they ended up with amounts to an international collection.

Before leaving the museum, step out onto the enclosed porch where you'll find the National Maritime Hall of Fame, immortalizing great mariners and ships from the Merchant Marine's history. Also, ask to see the little circular gallery, whose Tiffany window depicts Pan playing his pipes.

Incidentally, if you think the flagpole dominating the quadrangle looks tall, know that it's actually the largest in the world, featured in the Guinness book of World Records. Also, in front of O'Hara Hall, is the original eagle from Pennsylvania Station. And walk over to Wylie Hall, the former summer home of auto tycoon Walter P. Chrysler, which functions today as an administration building. Originally built by retail magnate Henri Bendel, the house was sold to Chrysler after Bendel's daughter drowned on the property.

Inside, you'll find some magnificent art works, including an enormous painting by Hunter Wood depicting sailors in a lifeboat guided to safety by a vision of Christ.

Important Information

Garvies Point Museum & Preserve
Barry Drive
Glen Cove
516-571-8010

Open: Tuesday to Saturday, 10 a.m. to 4 p.m., Sunday, 1 p.m. to 4 p.m., opens at 10 a.m. between Memorial Day and Labor Day; closed Mondays
Fee: $1 adults, 50 cents children
Tours: Self-guided; guided tours for educational programs
Rest rooms: Yes
On-site food: Picnic tables outdoors
Wheelchair access: Museum is accessible; trails are limited in access
Gift shop: Yes

Child appropriate: Yes

**Sands-Willets House
(Cow Neck Peninsula Historical Society)**
336 Port Washington Blvd.
Port Washington
516-365-9074

Open: Tuesdays and Wednesdays, 10 a.m. to 4 p.m., Sunday, 2 p.m. to 5 p.m.; other days by appointment only
Fee: $2.50 adults, $1 children under 12
Tours: Yes
Rest rooms: Yes
On-site food: No
Wheelchair access: No
Gift shop: Yes
Child appropriate: Yes

**American Merchant Marine Museum
at the U.S. Merchant Marine Academy**
Steamboat Road
Kings Point
516-773-5515

Open: Tuesday to Friday, 10 a.m. to 3 p.m., Saturday and Sunday, 1 p.m. to 4:30 p.m.; closed Mondays, all federal holidays, and the month of July
Fee: Donations
Tours: Informal self-guided tours; groups by appointment only. Audio boxes available at some exhibits
Rest rooms: Information unavailable
On-site food: Buffet-style lunch available at Officers Club on Wednesdays only (except school holidays) from 12:30 p.m. to 1 p.m., call 773-5340 for information; Seafarer (snack bar) on academy grounds, open weekdays only until 2 p.m.
Wheelchair access: Main floor only; restrooms not accessible
Gift shop: No
Child appropriate: Yes

Where to Eat

Land of Smiles
105 Middle Neck Rd.
Great Neck
516-773-6344
With its wallet-friendly prices, this unassuming but attractive little Thai restaurant in the heart of Great Neck really lives up to its name. For those who fear

the incendiary, don't worry — the kitchen will adjust the level of spiciness to your specifications. Flavors are clear, lively, harmonious. Lunch, by the way, is an especially good buy.

Gonzalo & Joe's American Cafe
5 School St.
Glen Cove
516-656-0003
This winning little Glen Cove bistro elevates home cooking to an art. The menu is simple, straightforward, and executed with consummate flair. Even something as humble as the french fried potato is done from scratch and wonderful. Sandwiches — such as the blackened chicken BLT or pulled pork — excel, as do salads, entrees, and desserts.

Stresa
1524 Northern Blvd.
Manhasset
516-365-6956
If you want to put a little elegance into your day, then this exquisite Manhasset ristorante is where to find it. The Italian fare — accorded four stars by Newsday's Peter Gianotti — is topnotch, and, at lunch, served weekdays only, is surprisingly moderate in price.

THE STONY BROOK ROUTE

If ever there were a Long Island historical gold mine, then the Three Village-Smithtown area is such. In fact, there's almost too much to see on this tour, which is why we leave the process of elimination to you. Deepwells, for instance, which is open for theatrical teas by reservations only, is a definite plan-ahead site. If you're going there, then you certainly won't want to stop for tea (sans theatrics) at the Caleb Smith House. To fit all this in in a more leisurely way, you might want to consider a two-day tour.

Thompson House

At the meticulously restored residence of the prominent Brookhaven Thompson family, you'll find the life of the 18th Century depicted with uncanny accuracy, based on painstaking studies of old inventories and records. The house reflects the year 1748, when three generations shared the home: grandparents Samuel and Hannah Thompson, Samuel's son Jonathan and his wife, Mary, and their children, Mary, Samuel, Isaac, Jonathan and baby Hannah.

The clapboard and shingle you see on the outside is the original exterior. Enter the hall, used as a kitchen and dining area, and you'll find the hearth seemingly ready for cooking; at the table, the pewter treenware service is laid out, waiting, it would seem, for the family to sit down.

In the room where the laundry was done, you'll see the implements of heavy-duty household chores — a spinning wheel, some barrels and a butter churn.

In the small downstairs bedroom, where

Newsday Photo / Thomas A. Ferrara

Actresses in 'Mrs. Gaynor's 1905 Tea Party' at Deepwells

grandparents Samuel and Hannah may have slept, the bed folds away; rooms then were multi-purpose affairs. The chamberpot you see there is a reproduction.

Not surprisingly, the center of family life was the combination parlor and bedroom. Note the lovely reproduction floorcloth, the rich bed hangings, and the beautiful Dutch kas or wardrobe where linens were kept.

The attic contains the quarters where the slaves (research has documented seven) slept, under the eaves. Look closely, and you can see the original mortar.

Outside, check out the pretty herb garden, maintained by the North Country Garden Club, before making the uphill climb to the little cemetery where members of the family are buried.

The Museums at Stony Brook

Unique and sophisticated, this Stony Brook attraction is, as its name indicates, actually several museums in one: a carriage house, an art museum, a Long Island history gallery, and a collection of 18th- and 19th-Century outbuildings. One might easily spend half a day here.

At the Dorothy and Ward Melville Carriage House, you'll find the enormous and artfully displayed collection of vehicles (many with real-looking horses) is among the finest in this part of the world. The centerpiece of the first floor is the huge, colorful Grace Darling Omnibus. This 1880 group vehicle was used by the St. Paul's school in Concord, N.H. A light box in front of the wagon shows the process of its restoration. To the left, you'll find the rooms that house the ornate European collection, much of it in original mint condition. Then, walk down the ramp to the displays downstairs. One, called "Carriages in Industrial America," showcases utilitarian vehicles: a tea wagon, a grocery wagon and the like. In another room, you'll find two magnificently painted gypsy wagons, from between 1860 and 1885. Inside of one, you can see the living quarters.

Another gallery is devoted to pleasure-driving vehicles, such as the elegant phaeton. The accompanying collection of clothing and accoutrements evokes days of grace and refinement. In yet another room check out the 1880 chariot d'Orsay, once owned by William K. Vanderbilt.

A room full of shiny red firefighting vehicles will delight children. They'll be especially taken with the 1875 hand-drawn exhibition vehicle, with its enormous gold wheels, as well as with the dazzling red-wheeled 1874 steam pump.

Outside, walk about the grounds, pausing to inhale the fragrance of the museum's herb garden. Then, stop into the 1877 Nassakeag Schoolhouse from South Setauket, with its wood-burning stove and old-fashioned desks with slates. When you visit the mid-19th-Century blacksmith shop, you may be fortunate enough to catch one of the occasional demonstrations on the use of the forge. The 1794 Barn and Carriage shed, the oldest structure on the grounds, holds a collection of antique tools. Children will enjoy climbing on an 1870 farm vehicle.

In the Art Museum, you'll find some of the works of Long Island's illustrious Mount family, the most celebrated of whom is painter William Sidney Mount (1807-1868). Mount's works depicted everyday life on Long Island. On those rare occasions that Mount's works are on loan to other museums, the paintings of his brother, Shepard

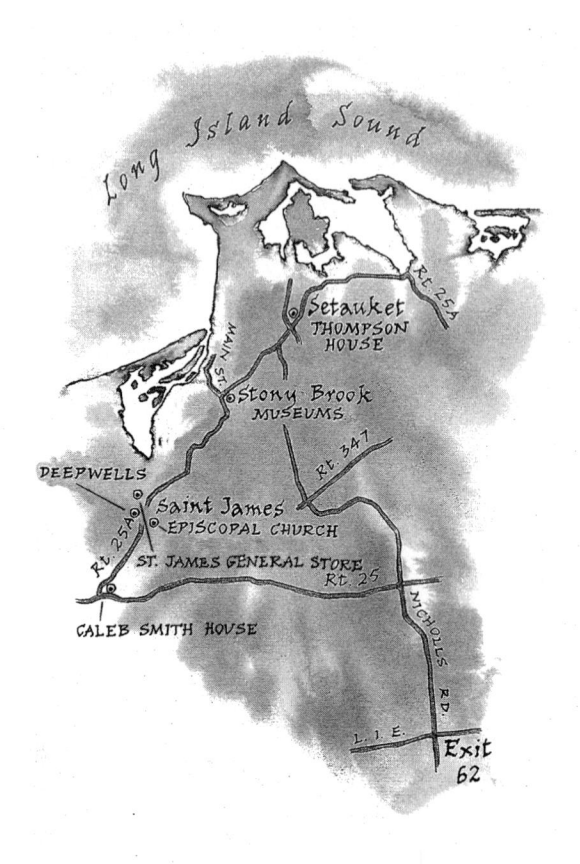

Directions

To Thompson House
Long Island Expressway to exit 62; go north on County Road 97 (Nicolls Road) to its end. Turn right onto Route 25A, which becomes Main Street, and turn left on North Country Road. House is on east side of the road.

To The Museums at Stony Brook
From Thompson House, return to Route 25A, making a right. Proceed west until Main Street. Turn left; museum parking lot is on the right.

To St. James Episcopal Church
From museums, turn right out of parking lot, continuing into St. James; church is on the left.

To Deepwells, St. James General Store
From church, make left out of parking lot; Deepwells is ahead on the right. Store is adjacent to property.

To Caleb Smith House
From Deepwells, turn right out of parking lot on to North Country Road, go to Route 25; house is on left.

Alonzo Mount (1804-1868) are often exhibited. Across the street, in the History Museum, you can visit the decoy gallery, which chronicles duck hunting on Long Island via photographs, art, and carved decoys. A series of miniature rooms, made during the 1940s by artisan Frederick Hicks, illustrates the history of decorative interiors from the 16th Century to the 1930s. Children may not be the only ones who find themselves drawn into these tiny, ingeniously fashioned scenes.

St. James Episcopal Church

St. James is the only community on Long Island that's named for one of its churches. And this is no ordinary church. Designed by Richard Upjohn, the prominent church architect who also designed Trinity Church in Manhattan, the charming Gothic Revival wood structure was built in 1853; its narthex and tower were added during the 1870s. Among the church's most prominent parishoners was architect Stanford White, who designed three of its stained glass windows.

The window which depicts the theme of the Good Shephard is one of two signed Tiffany pieces (the other is a memorial plaque in a connecting wing). Perhaps even more beautiful is the Minott Memorial window, done in wonderful pastel hues of lilac and pink and white and signed Lederle-Geissler. The windows designed by White include the Nicoll Clinch Memorial window on the south wall. A plaque also is dedicated to the memory of James Clinch Smith, who perished on the Titanic and was the brother of White's wife, Bessie Smith White.

Outside, walk through the cemetery, which is on the National Register of Historic Places. Most renowned among the buried is Stanford White, who was murdered in Manhattan by the jealous husband of his paramour, Evelyn Nesbit. White's gravestone is easily found; the tallest structure in the cemetery, it consists of a striking white tower gracefully topped with a carved shell. A monument most fitting.

Deepwells

Would you like to have tea with John or Ethel Barrymore? How about overhearing some spicy chit-chat about Stanford White and Evelyn Nesbit. All this is possible at Deepwells, the charming Victorian mansion, owned by Suffolk County and operated by the nonprofit Friends for Long Island Heritage.

Call in advance, and you can arrange to attend

Newsday Photo / J. Michael Dombroski
The St. James General Store, in business since 1857

one of the highly entertaining theatrical teas, each designed around an original play whose characters, local historical notables, are decked out in full period regalia and interact with audience members.

Perhaps Mrs. William Gaynor, the lady of the house, will greet you at the door, while her maid passes hors d'oeuvres, the music from an old Victrola playing gently in the background.

The main part of the tea, which costs about $25, will take place in a lovely Victorian parlor whose mural depicts local scenery in soft colors.

St. James General Store

Understand, this isn't just any old emporium; it's believed to be the oldest continually operating general store in the United States. Under the same auspices as Deepwells, the St. James General Store, has been doing business since Ebenezer Smith first hung out his shingle in 1857.

Appropriately, the store's upper shelves display artifacts and antiques from Smith's day. The original kerosene lamps you see have been converted to electricity and use copies of original Edison bulbs. At first, the General Store functioned as the town post office, and, to this day, continues to offer postal services. You can bring packages to be mailed to the counter, a counter scarred by years when customers struck their matches on its well-worn surface. In the store's heydey, folks would gather around the old potbellied stove to catch up on local gossip. The back room is the oldest section. Here, you'll see the old bronze cash register, as well as the store's original phone, still in working order.

Of course, you can shop here. Upstairs is a bookstore, while, throughout the shop, all kinds of items are for sale, some having to do with Victorian times, others relating to contemporary Long Island. Before leaving, pick up a pamphlet outlining the local driving tour, which leaves from the store. If you've got the time, the leisurely drive is well worth taking.

Caleb Smith House

George Washington didn't sleep here, but he did stop to rest his horses next door, at the Widow Blydenburgh's Tavern, where the Smithtown Public Library is now. It all happened in 1790, when he stopped en route from Setauket to Oyster Bay.

Expanded in 1819, it was moved to its present location in 1955. (This house belonged to the son Caleb. His father, Caleb Smith, lived in the house that is part of Caleb Smith State Park.) This house, also known as Caleb Smith II House functions not only as a local landmark but also as an antique shop, tearoom and headquarters of the Smithtown Historical Society. Here, two distinct historical periods are represented. There's the 18th-Century portion of the house, which probably started out as a simple salt box. To this, Caleb Smith added two parlors to the front and back. The furniture you see was donated by members of the Smith and Blydenburgh families. Note the portraits of Bessie Smith and her sister Ella, aged 4 and 8, done by artist Shepherd Alonzo Mount. Bessie eventually married architect Stanford White.

Upstairs, in the older part of the house, you'll see one furnished bedroom showcasing a little carriage, a child's walker, a loom, and dollhouse furniture. There's a lovely sleigh bed as well as some wonderful old costumes. If you come on a Friday, you can, for a small tariff, enjoy an old-fashioned tea.

Important Information

Thompson House
91 North Country Rd.
Setauket
516-692-4664

Open: Memorial Day through Columbus Day, Friday to Sunday, 1 p.m.to 5 p.m.
Fee: $3 adults, $1.50 children and seniors
Tours: Yes
Rest rooms: Yes
On-site food: No
Wheelchair access: Partial
Gift shop: No
Child appropriate: Yes

The Museums at Stony Brook
1208 Rte. 25A
Stony Brook
516-751-0066

Open: July, August, December, Monday to Saturday, 10 a.m. to 5 p.m.; Sunday, noon to 5 p.m.; all other months, Wednesday to Saturday, 10 a.m. to 5 p.m.; Sunday, noon to 5 p.m.
Fee: $4 adults, $3 seniors 60 and older, $2 students 6-17 and college students with identification; children under 6 and museum members, free; college students with identification free on Wednesday
Tours: By appointment and reduced rate group tours
Rest rooms: Yes
On-site food: No
Wheelchair access: Yes
Gift shop: Yes
Child appropriate: Yes

St. James Episcopal Church
490 North Country Rd.
St. James
516-584-5560

Open: Monday to Friday, 9:30 a.m. to 2:30 p.m.
Fee: Free
Tours: No
Rest rooms: Yes (if office is open)
On-site food: No
Wheelchair access: Yes
Gift shop: No
Child appropriate: Older children

Deepwells
Rte. 25A
St. James
516-862-6080

Open: For special events as scheduled

Fee: Varies according to program
Tours: By appointment
Rest rooms: Yes
On-site food: Yes
Wheelchair access: Yes
Gift shop: Yes
Child appropriate: Yes

St. James General Store
516 Moriches Rd.
St. James
516-862-8333

Open: Daily, 10 a.m. to 5 p.m.
Fee: None
Tours: By appointment
Rest rooms: No
On-site food: Some food items for sale
Wheelchair access: No
Gift shop: Yes
Child appropriate: Yes

Caleb Smith House (Smithtown Historical Society)
5 North Country Rd.
Smithtown
516-265-6768

Open: Monday to Friday, 9 a.m. to 4 p.m., Saturday, noon to 4 p.m.
Fee: Donation
Tours: Yes
Rest rooms: Yes
On-site food: Tea 2-4 p.m. Fridays (reservations required)
Wheelchair access: No
Gift shop: Yes (consignment shop)
Child appropriate: Older children

Where to Eat

Bella Vita City Grill
430 North Country Rd.
St. James
516-862-8060
Flatbreads — inventive little pizzas with cracker-thin crusts — are the specialty at this snappy Italianate cafe. Pastas are also a good bet, as are the sandwiches and salads. You can be assured of finding a burger on the midday menu.

Curry Club
766 Rte. 25A
Stony Brook
516-751-4845
The big bargain around town is the all-inclusive buffet luncheon offered at this friendly Indian eatery. Even if you go the a la carte route, you won't break the bank; you will, however, get a lot of flavor for the money.

Green Cactus Grill
1099 Rte. 25A
Stony Brook
516-751-0700
Ideal for the light-bite pick-me-up, this order-at-the-counter tacqueria offers a lively assortment of salsas to accompany their freshly grilled, tortilla-wrapped meats and vegetables. Given the prices, it's no wonder that the place draws a large college following.

Three Village Inn
150 Main St.
Stony Brook
516-751-0555
The early American charm of Stony Brook is embodied by the near-legendary Three Village Inn, a restaurant that hasn't allowed its popularity to interfere with quality. Although prices are somewhat high for lunch (expect to spend between $15 and $20 per person), the fare is well-executed and served by staff members attired in Colonial garb. A table with a view of the harbor is a must.

OLD RIVERHEAD

The Town of Riverhead harbors lots more than a behemoth outlet center and the Suffolk County seat. Here, midway between rolling farmlands and glamorous resorts, is a municipality whose diverse and interesting culture straddles the rural and the urban. A multitude of surprises awaits the visitor.

Hallockville Farm and Folklife Center

The life of a North Fork farm family in the 19th Century is what you'll see at Hallockville Farm and Folklife Center. The oldest of the several buildings on the grounds, the Hallock Homestead, was built in 1765. But it is the time period between 1880-1910, that serves as the museum's focal point.

You'll enter at the Hudson House, which was moved in 1988 from its original site — about a mile away — to where it stands today. Built by Samuel Terry Hudson during the 1840s, the house currently functions as an educational center for the museum.

Begin your tour at the barn, a pegged post and beam construction which was built about 1765 but moved to its present site by the Hallock family in 1866. Outside, introduce yourself to the museum's two cows, Nettie and Emma, recent arrivals. Inside, you'll see a variety of tools and implements, including a bicyclelike cultivator, said to have been invented by Hudson. Here, too, is everything you might ever need to scrape the hair off a newly slaughtered pig. Afterwards, visit the corn crib, where corn was separated and ground into flour. There's a chicken coop, an old four-seat outhouse, and a smokehouse (sometimes used) where the scent of smoked hams, eels, and fish seems to linger.

In the Hallock house itself, you'll see many of the original rugs and furnishings. Before entering, check out the shoemaker's shop and the milk cellar, both testimony to the unavaiability of shops and services we take for granted. Inside, the

Newsday Photo / John H. Cornell Jr.

A 1905 Oldsmobile Curved Dash Runabout

kitchen is equipped with an iron stove as well as a tub for boiling clothes. An ancestor to the modern crock pot was kept hot by using heated rocks.

For the Hallock family, music was a major form of entertainment; the ornate Victorian family dining room has a piano, the East Parlor, used for informal gatherings of family and friends, has an old Victrola, and the more formal West Parlor, used for funerals, weddings and social gatherings, is furnished with its own organ.

On your way up the staircase, check out the cranberry-glass fixture, which is made with 22-karat gold. In the master bedroom, you'll find a wonderful old trunk filled with antique clothing. In the little girl's room, there are tiny shoes by the bed; you'll also see a sewing machine. The boys' room, equipped with a bathtub, has antlers on the wall, used for hanging hats.

If you're wondering, the last Hallock to occupy the house was Ella, who lived there until 1979.

Railroad Museum of Long Island at Riverhead

Within whistling distance of the Riverhead Long Island Rail Road station, in an antiquated looking train yard, you'll find a collection of wonderful old railroad cars, most of which are open for touring.

Among the cars on display is Steam Locomotive #39, which ran from 1929-1955 on the Oyster Bay Branch. The centerpiece of the collection is the 1932 Bi-Level #200. It was a prototype for all the double-deckers built in this country and the first all-aluminum train made. Although approximately 300 similar trains were built, the car you see here is the only surviving one of its kind. If you've got the time, the museum offers even more railroad cars, displays and a gift shop at its Greenport branch.

Suffolk County Historical Society

This old-fashioned, museum-lover's museum is a treasure chest of county lore. Founded in 1886, the Historical Society has been a fine place to find refuge on a rainy day, to bring curious kids, to browse. The Greek Revival-Federal building, constructed in 1930, was listed on the National Register of Historic Places in 1994.

On the first floor, in addition to a changing exhibit, you'll find a room devoted to the history of the American Indians of Eastern Long Island, with tools, beads, pottery, and eating vessels, including an old mortar and pestle in remarkably good condition. You'll learn about the Indians' contact with missionaries and meet some celebrated East End American Indians from the 19th Century, such as the noted Stephen (Talkhouse) Pharaoh. Craft work done by contemporary Indians from surrounding areas is also displayed.

Next door is a fascinating artifact and furniture gallery. One can't help but be drawn to the rather primitive-looking painting of the Conklin children of Greenport, which was done by an anonymous painter about 1854. It's fun to study the painting in order to match up some of the items of clothing and toys on display in a showcase filled with Conklin family memorabilia on the other side of the room. There's also a circa 1905 portrait of Grace Floyd Delafield Robinson, a benefactor of the museum and a descendent of William Floyd. In the main hallway, look for the museum's portrait of Floyd; like the painting displayed at his estate in Mastic, this, too, is a copy of the Peale original.

Downstairs, in the gallery entitled, "Early Suffolk Transportation," check out the collection of blacksmith's tools, the 1860 farm wagon, the 1880 market and pleasure wagon, and the two sleighs, one an 1800 Portland-style cutter, and the other a two-seat country sleigh. There also are two 19th-Century bicycles. Without a doubt, the showpiece of the exhibit is the marvelous 1905 Oldsmobile. How fragile it looks today; how beautiful, too.

Lining the downstairs hallway is a charming series of miniature rooms, each depicting a different historical scene. All were done as part of the WPA project during the 1930s. On an opposite wall is a collection of half-models of boats, all made by Long Island's master boatmaker, Gil Smith.

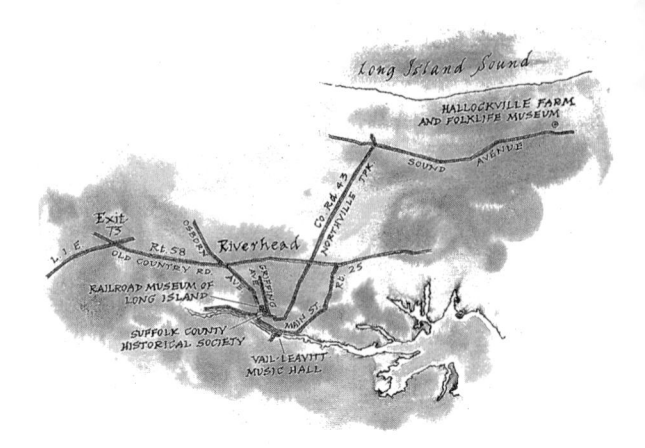

Directions

To Hallockville Farm and Folklife Museum
Long Island Expressway to end (exit 73); stay on Route 58 (Old Country Road) through traffic circle to where you see K mart and BJ's on right; turn left onto Northville Turnpike (County Road 43). Proceed on Northville to Sound Avenue and turn right. Continue about 3½ miles to museum, which is on left.

To Railroad Museum of Long Island
From Hallockville, go west on Sound Avenue, turn left at Northville Turnpike to where road ends. Turn left onto Roanoke Avenue, take immediate right onto Railroad Avenue. At next stop sign make right onto Griffing Ave. Parking lot on left.

To Suffolk County Historical Society
From Railroad museum, go west to Osborn Avenue, make left and go to Main Street, make right. Museum is right there.

To Vail-Leavitt Music Hall
Proceed east on Route 25 to Peconic Avenue and turn right; theater is on left (parking on right).

A museum detailing the history of Suffolk County would hardly be complete without a whaling exhibit, and the one here is quite impressive. You'll see harpoons, a ship's log, and a showcase on toothed and baleen whales. Also included are examples of whaler's arts — several pieces of scrimshaw as well as a lovely mahogany and whale-ivory watch case in the shape of a building.

Another room details the agricultural life of the

county, with farm implements, baskets, tinsmithing and leatherworks, among other things. Military history buffs will enjoy the "war room" whose display includes rifles, a real Civil War uniform, as well as a dandy New York State Militia dragoon-style helmet. Those who prefer gentler, more domestic arts can go back upstairs to admire the fine collection of ceramics — including some wonderful Staffordshire and tea sets.

The Vail-Leavitt Music Hall

Here's a little secret: there's a jewel box hidden away in Riverhead's busy downtown. It's called the Vail-Leavitt Music Hall, and it's situated upstairs from the Mini-Cine on Peconic Avenue. Built in 1881 by lumber merchants David and George Vail, the theater is lovely — horseshoe-shaped, with gilt trim, crystal chandeliers, a wonderful painted stage curtain, and elegant upper galleries and box seats.

It also boasts an historical connection to Thomas Alva Edison, which is why you see his portrait hanging in the rear. Shortly after its opening, the theater became one of the first public venues to utilize the electric light bulb, an event which took place during a presentation of "Uncle Tom's Cabin."

In 1908, the music hall was the site of the Great Edison Show, a silent moving picture detailing the sensational murder of architect Stanford White; it was a tremendous hit.

In 1909, the theater was purchased by Simon Leavitt, who leased it to showman Franklin P. McCutcheon, who, in 1914, brought an experimental talking picture show — advertised as "The Eighth Wonder of the World" — to the theater.

During World War I, the theater continued to show movies and vaudeville acts but fell into decline over the ensuing years. Ultimately, the site was converted into a Chinese restaurant which, in 1925, closed because of a kitchen fire. The theater then became a pool hall as well as betting parlor, until finally, Leavitt's son, clothier Theodore Leavitt, closed it.

Now, thanks to the Council for the Vail-Leavitt Music Hall, a corporation formed by Riverhead citizens, the theater has been restored to near-mint condition. Once sufficient funds have been raised to complete the restoration of the balcony and install an adequate sprinkler system, Riverhead may witness the elaborate curtain rising for a performance.

Important Information

Hallockville Farm and Folklife Museum
6038 Sound Ave.
Riverhead
516-298-5292

Open: April 1 to Dec. 15, Wednesday to Saturday, 11 a.m. to 4 p.m., Sunday, noon to 4 p.m.; rest of year by appointment only
Fee: $3 adults, $2 students and seniors, children under 6 free
Tours: Yes
Rest rooms: Portable
On-site food: During special events
Wheelchair access: Not in house and barn
Gift shop: Yes
Child appropriate: Yes

Railroad Museum of Long Island (Riverhead branch)
Griffing and Railroad Avenues
Riverhead Railroad Station
Riverhead
516-727-7920

Open: Saturday, 10 a.m. to 4 p.m.
Fee: $1 adults, 50 cents children
Tours: Yes
Rest rooms: No
On-site food: No
Wheelchair access: No
Gift shop: No
Child appropriate: Yes

Suffolk County Historical Society
300 W. Main St.
Riverhead
516-727-2881

Open: Tuesday to Saturday, 12:30 p.m. to 4:30 p.m.
Fee: Free
Tours: By appointment only for groups
Rest rooms: Yes
Open-site food: No
Wheelchair access: No
Gift shop: Weathervane Gift Shop
Child appropriate: Yes

Vail-Leavitt Music Hall
18 Peconic Ave.
Riverhead
516-727-5782

Open: Tours every evening following a movie

showing at Mini Cine downstairs; occasional weekday tours; call for hours. Other tours during Riverhead festivals and, on weekend afternoons, by appointment
Fee: Free (donations welcomed)
Tours: Yes
Rest rooms: In Mini-Cine downstairs
On-site food: Movie fare downstairs
Wheelchair access: No
Gift shop: Items available for sale
Child appropriate: Older children

Where to Eat

Spicy's Barbecue
225 W. Main St.
Riverhead
516-727-2781
Don't expect luxury here. But if you've got a yen for topnotch barbecued ribs served with a dandy mustard-enhanced midwestern-style barbecue sauce, look no further. Greaselessly deep-fried chicken is another standout. Finish with a slice of fluffy sweet potato pie.

Jazzy Brown's
17 E. Main St.
Riverhead
516-369-4408
If buffet-style doesn't bother you , you can snag the soul-food bargain of the East End. Everything is homey, old-fashioned, and flavor-intense. Desserts, such as hummingbird cake, are wonderful.

Star Confectionery
4 Main St.
Riverhead
516-727-9873
This is just a luncheonette, but it's been around forever — a good sign. They've got high-quality sandwiches, and the homemade ice-cream is tops.

Hy Ting
58 W. Main St.
Riverhead
516-727-1557
A dimly-lit Chinese restaurant whose perfectly ordinary menu is done with extraordinary elan. Most lunches, complete with soup and salad, are generously portioned and ultra-satisfying.

COLD SPRING HARBOR AND LLOYD NECK

Bring along a camera for this tour, for you'll surely want to remember some of the spectacular coastline vistas around the Lloyd Neck area. As for the quaint village of Cold Spring Harbor, it is as the saying goes, picture perfect. Between snapshots, you gain fascinating insights into the area's past, for this history-steeped locale has lots more going for it than just a pretty face.

Joseph Lloyd House

No, George Washington did not sleep here. But Jupiter Hammond, America's first published black poet, lived and worked in the shingled Georgian home that overlooks the waters of Lloyd Harbor.

Before touring the house, you'll see a small exhibit on Hammond. Some believe he was taught to read and write by someone in the Lloyd family, while others maintain he learned simply by reading the Bible.

The house was built in 1766, a time when most homes tended to be cramped affairs with low ceilings. This home, however, was a veritable mansion. Having immigrated from England, James Lloyd, the family patriarch and a Boston merchant, married Griselda Sylvester, who was the owner of the property upon which the manor was built. During those times, it was uncommon for a woman to own land, since males traditionally were the ones to inherit. But Sylvester had been engaged to a sea captain; before he'd shipped out, all the pre-nuptial legalities, such as the signing over of properties into the names of both husband and

Newsday Photo / Bill Davis

The slaves' quarters at the Joseph Lloyd House

wife, had been completed. When the captain was lost at sea, Sylvester, although unmarried, received the property. After James Lloyd married her, he bought the rest of the land in the area now known as Lloyd Neck. Later, his four grandsons divided the property into four parts. His grandson Joseph built the house we see today.

But the American Revolution wrought havoc upon the grandsons of James Lloyd. Brothers Henry and James were pro-English while brothers Joseph and John were pro-Colonist. During the time that Huntington was occupied by British, Joseph and John waited out the war with relatives in New England. About a year before the war turned in favor of the Colonists, Joseph learned of the British victory at Charleston, S.C., and in despair, committed suicide. Later, Joseph's nephew John returned and took over the property.

The Lloyds were traders and merchants. John put in a dock at the end of the property, on the site where singer-composer Billy Joel later made his home for a time. For many years, the Lloyds operated a steamboat landing known as Lloyd's Dock for the transportation of freight and passengers to New York but when the Long Island Rail Road came to Huntington, the era of Lloyd prosperity ended. After the family lost the property, two other families owned the house. The last owner, Anne Wood, had received the house as a wedding gift from her father. She lived to almost 100, putting in the beautiful old-fashioned garden. Charles Lindbergh, in fact, rented it for nearly two years. Before Wood died, she bequeathed the property to the Society for the Preservation of Long Island Antiquities.

Today, the kitchen is much the same as it was when John Lloyd came back after the American Revolution. Everything you see is based upon an

Directions
(map on opposite page)

To Joseph Lloyd Manor House
Long Island Expressway to exit 49 (Route 110), go north to Route 25A, make left and proceed to West Neck Road, make right and take through causeway, which will bring you to Lloyd Neck; house will be on left on bluff.

To Cold Spring Harbor Whaling Museum
From Lloyd Manor House, take West Neck Road to Huntington. Turn right on Route 25A (Main Street) in Huntington village. Go west to Cold Spring Harbor. Museum is on the right, just before Cold Spring Harbor.

To the Gallery of The Society for the Preservation of Long Island Antiquities
From Whaling Museum, proceed west on Route 25A; gallery is on your right, just past the shops but before the park.

To Cold Spring Harbor Fish Hatchery and Aquarium
From gallery, proceed west on Route 25A, bearing right (following road) at Route 108 intersection; Hatchery will be on left.

To St. John's Episcopal Church
Park at hatchery, walk to church located directly behind it.

---

inventory compiled at John's death. The paint, a dark teal green, is the original color, arrived at by stripping down the walls' fifteen coats. As the story goes, when restorers got down to the final coat, the room was suffused with the smell of apples, a cooking staple whose fragrance probably pervaded the Lloyd kitchen during the 18th Century. The room also has its original hearth, fireplace and oven, as well as cooking tools of the period.

In the parlor, you'll find a copy of the original carpet, which was described in the inventory. The office, done in several shades of green, is where John conducted business. The bright green desk is an original. There are several authentic documents here, as well as a coat from the period.

Upstairs, the parlor utilizes lots of contrasting fabrics, a common decorating practice of the day. The wallpaper, a reproduction, was modeled after an actual scrap of paper. The room next door has a sloping floor and a rope bed, complete with keys for tightening the ropes to sleep more comfortably.

In another section thought by some to be slaves' quarters, sleeping bags are stored. There is a spinning wheel, but no fireplace, a sad comment about the prevailing sensibility toward slaves.

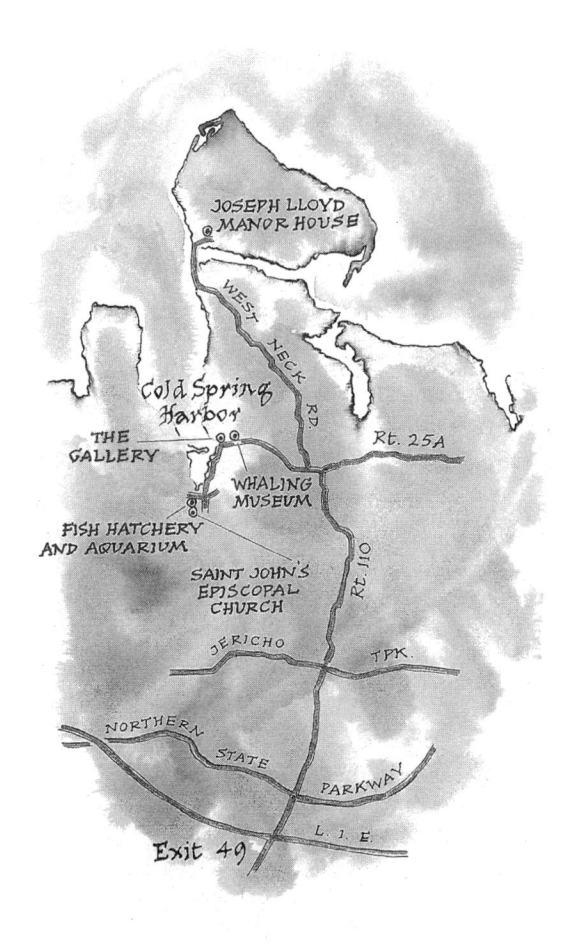

Conclude the tour by visiting the Victorian wing, added by Mrs. Wood. And don't forget to see the garden, with its beautiful water view. Here, you'll find boxwood, apple trees, beautifully manicured hedges, a rose arbor, ivy, and, at the center, a sundial.

Cold Spring Harbor Whaling Museum

Driven by the desire to make the area's whaling and maritime heritage understandable on every level, the Cold Spring Harbor Whaling Museum has gone out of its way to gear its exhibits to every age group. And quite a job it's done. Take a self-guided tour, with the help of an audio tape, and the collection of whale-related items comes sharply into focus.

A genuine 19th-Century whale boat, 30 feet long, comes from the whaling ship Daisy, built in Setauket in 1872. The boat came into the possession of Robert Cushman Murphy, a curator at the Museum of Natural History who had, earlier, gone out on the Daisy on a whaling expedition. It was on that voyage that he took the photographs you'll see displayed behind the boat itself.

On the audio tour, you'll learn about that particular boat as well as the entire village of Cold Spring Harbor. The tour begins at the large and meticulously wrought diorama of the town about 1850. You'll find out why today's Main Street used to be called Bedlam Street (there's a boutique in the village by that name today). Whaling, you'll learn, was perhaps the first fully integrated industry in America. Who are the Jones brothers and what role did they play in the development of whaling in Cold Spring Harbor? On the tour, you'll find out.

In the Wonder of Whales room, a killer whale's skull is exhibited next to the skull of a mouse. While clearly differing in size, the two are surprisingly similar in other ways. You'll also learn about the two kinds of whale, those with and without teeth. And you can listen to the hypnotic sounds of a humpbacked whale.

There's a model of the whaling ship Bartholomew Gosnold. Learn all about life on a whaling expedition — the bad food, the bad smells — as well as the meaning of the cry "she blows" and the phrase "Nantucket sleigh ride."

The main room holds some striking examples of scrimshaw. Sailors also created art out of shells, such as the touching "sailor's Valentine" you'll see on display. The museum features interesting videos on whaling, and it also holds weekend programs for families in a large education room that has, instead of a rocking horse, a rocking whale.

For some, the killing of whales seems cruel. But while the exhibits do take us back to the old whaling days of the 19th Century, when whaling was an accepted means of earning a livelihood, the Cold Spring Harbor Whaling Museum is firm in its commitment to educate the public toward conservation of today's remaining whales.

The Gallery
(The Society for the Preservation
of Long Island Antiquities)

At Long Island's most active force in preserving and making accessible historic sites, you can find exhibits that change regularly. They're always interesting and always focus on Long Island. Call to find out what's currently on display.

A brook trout in a tank at the Cold Spring Harbor fish hatchery
Newsday Photo / Ken Spencer

Cold Spring Harbor Fish Hatchery and Aquarium

Although this attraction may seem a detour from the strictly historical, this 115-year old hatchery was declared a National Historic Landmark several years ago. Besides, no trip to Cold Spring Harbor is ever considered complete without a brief stop at the Fish Hatchery. If you're touring with kids, they will thank you for including it on your itinerary.

Start at the large brick Walter L. Ross Building, where you'll see baby turtles, and large fish — salmon, sturgeon, and trout — all native to New York. The turtles, all of which have been incubated and hatched on premises, are particularly engaging.

Outside, the aquaculture hatcheries raise as many as 120,000 trout a year, which are sold to the public as well as to municipalities and sportsmen's clubs wishing to stock ponds and lakes.

In the various ponds, you'll find trout in different stages of development and a warm water pond stocked with large ornamental fish as well as a turtle pond.

And be sure to ask for Junior, the Hatchery's resident snapping turtle who is between 80 and 100 years old, weighing in at over 75 pounds.

The small Fairchild Building houses what the Hatchery says is the largest collection of fresh water amphibians in New York State.

Spend a few minutes in the company of frogs, water snakes, and salamanders.

St. John's Episcopal Church

If you're touring on a weekday, you might want to walk behind the fish hatchery. There, you'll see a small white pondside church so picturesque that it was featured in the wedding scene of the movie "In and Out." Founded in 1835, St. John's Episcopal is worth visiting, especially to see the three dreamily impressionistic stained glass Tiffany windows on the eastern wall. On the right is the pastel-hued Moore Memorial window, entitled the "Angel of Resurrection." In the center, the John Divine Jones Memorial window, whose theme is "The Good Shepherd,' provides a study in cool blues and greens. The north window, the Townsend Jones Memorial, depicts the "Annunciation" in lovely lavender and pink tones. Outside, enjoy the waterside vista.

Important Information

Joseph Lloyd Manor House
Lloyd Lane and Lloyd Harbor Rd.
Lloyd Harbor
516-692-4664

Open: Memorial Day to Columbus Day, Sundays only, 1 p.m. to 4 p.m.; groups and school programs by appointment
Fee: $3 adults, $1.50 senior citizens and children
Tours: Yes
Rest rooms: Yes
On-site food: No
Wheelchair access: Downstairs only
Gift shop: No
Child appropriate: Yes

Cold Spring Harbor Whaling Museum
Main Street
Cold Spring Harbor
516-367-3418

Open: Memorial Day to Labor Day, 7 days a week, 11 a.m. to 5 p.m., all other times, Tuesday to Sunday, 11 a.m. to 5 p.m.
Fee: $2 adults, $1.50 seniors and students 6-12; children 5 and under free
Tours: Yes, impromptu by interpreters. Audio tours also available
Rest rooms: Yes
On-site food: No
Wheelchair access: Yes
Gift shop: Yes
Child appropriate: Yes

The Gallery of The Society for the Preservation of Long Island Antiquities
Main Street and Shore Road
Cold Spring Harbor
516-367-6295

Open: May to December, Tuesday to Sunday, 11 a.m. to 4 p.m.
Fee: Donations accepted
Tours: No
Rest rooms: Yes
On-site food: No
Wheelchair access: Yes
Gift shop: Yes
Child appropriate: Older children

Cold Spring Harbor Fish Hatchery and Aquarium
Route 25A
Laurel Hollow
516-692-6768

Open: Daily, 10 a.m. to 5 p.m.; closed Thanksgiving Day and Christmas Day
Fee: $3 adults, $1.50 children 5-12 and people over 65; children under 5 free
Tours: Pre-arranged groups only
Rest rooms: Yes
On-site food: No
Wheelchair access: Yes
Gift shop: Yes
Child appropriate: Yes

St. John's Episcopal Church
Route 25A
Laurel Hollow
516-692-6368

Open: Year-round except July and August, Monday to Friday, 9 a.m. to noon and 1 p.m. to 4 p.m.; July and August, Monday to Friday, 9 a.m. to noon
Fee: Free
Tours: No
Rest rooms: Yes
On-site food: No
Wheelchair access: Yes
Gift shop: No
Child appropriate: Older children

Where to Eat

Trattoria Grasso Due
134 Main St.
Cold Spring Harbor
516-367-6060
At this Italianate cafe, pastas and salads are fine

choices for a relaxing meal. Here, the flavors are bright and the garlic rings true.

Imperial Hunan Szechuan
329 W. Main St.
Huntington
516-421-4726
The staff is hospitable and the Chinese food fine at this moderately priced spot in Huntington. Lunch, complete with soup and rice, will handily see you through a day's sightseeing.

Jonathan's Ristorante
15 Wall St.
Huntington
516-549-0055
You can always be assured of something stylish and well-prepared at this attractive trattoria in the heart of Huntington. This is not, however, a bargain-priced choice, so plan accordingly.

THE SOUTH SHORE GOLD COAST

Ask people what they know about Long Island's turn-of-the-century millionaires, and most would agree that any big-timer worth a polo pony owned an estate on the North Shore. Actually, Long Island had more than one Gold Coast. A surprising number of wealthy industrialists, attracted by the prospect of boating, sport-fishing, and summer fun built palatial summer homes along the South Shore's wetlands.

Although the glitter days on Long Island's South Shore are gone, some of the great estates, like Westbrook, (now the Bayard Cutting Arboretum) remain intact, open to the public. On this tour, we'll visit some of those estates, as well as the Southside Sportsman's Club where many of the millionaires fished, hunted and socialized. Plan on spending most of a day.

Bayard Cutting Arboretum

This well-treed estate, which some mistake for a place to get tree cuttings, happens to be named for its original owner, New York attorney and railroad magnate William Bayard Cutting.

Before moving to Oakdale, William Bayard Cutting held a membership in the Southside Sportsman's Club, where he'd frequently come to hunt and fish. Cutting enjoyed the club so much that he decided to build a country estate nearby. He bought the estate of George Lorillard and, in 1886 began work on the English Tudor-Queen Anne-

Newsday Photo / Daniel Goodrich
Stained-glass windows at the Bayard Cutting Arboretum

style estate he called Westbrook. The park-like grounds, with their extensive conifer collections and gardens, were designed by the architectural firm of Frederick Law Olmstead, the architect-landscaper known best for having designed Central Park.

In warmer weather, stroll around the grounds, taking in the pinetum walk, the wild flower walk, the rhododendron walk, the bird watchers' walk, and the swamp cypress walk. This is a place to indulge one's appreciation of flora and fauna.

The house, which has more than 60 rooms, is graced with magnificent woodwork and a number of Tiffany-stained glass windows, thanks to the fact that Louis Comfort Tiffany was a friend of Cutting and a fellow-member of the Southside Sportsman's Club. Although only a few rooms downstairs are open to the public, they're well worth seeing. The library, now used as a dining area for the adjacent snack bar, is adorned with a beautiful hand-carved Elizabethan oak fireplace. A must-see is the dining room, which has been restored to its original splendor, which you view in a photograph on display, showing the Cutting family having dinner at the same Chippendale table. Today, there's protective glass over the walls, which are covered in hand-sewn French Aubusson tapestry.

In the center hall, there's a dramatic and graceful 18th-Century sculpture of the Greek deity Silenius, a god of the woodlands. How appropriate an artifact for this lovely estate.

Long Island Maritime Museum

Housed in the former garage of Meadow Edge, the Anson Hard estate, designed by renowned South Shore architect Isaac Green, is a small museum dedicated to Long Island's maritime life. In the center hall, you'll see the St. Lawrence skiff that Commodore Frederick Bourne used to row his wife around the little lakes he'd dredged on the property next door. The museum's trophy room holds a variety of trophies from boat races. Don't miss the small photograph of Long Island's master boat builder Gil Smith.

In a gallery dedicated to the lifesaving stations of Long Island, you'll learn about the units set up along the coast for the purpose of aid and rescue in the all-too-frequent shipwrecks. On Feb. 8, 1895, the Louis V. Place sank. The very next day, lifesavers were again busy dealing with the wreckage of the John B. Manning.

Next walk over to the William P. Rudolph Oyster House, part of the world-renowned Blue Point oyster company and one of only two original oyster processing houses left on the east coast, the other being in Mystic Seaport in Connecticut. The story of the Blue Point oyster business, though, is actually the story of West Sayville's Dutch immigrants, who founded and worked the business. You'll meet many of them in a photographic exhibit on the wall, the most notable, perhaps, being Jacob Ockers, the man known as the Oyster King. Ockers' West Sayville home, now owned by the Town of Islip, is open to the public. Before leaving, take note of the skylights, which face west to enable workers to catch the rays of the afternoon sun.

On the grounds, you also can visit a working boat shop, which is open to the public on Saturday mornings. Outside, on the dock, check out some of the old boats tied up — the tugboat Charlotte and the houseboat Hildegarde, and ask about the stories connected to them. Finally, there's a quaint little bayman's cottage on the property. It belonged to the Beebe family and has been restored to mirror the era about 1880. The wainscoting, which covers the ceiling as well as the walls, is especially beautiful. In the parlor, you'll find a coal stove, an old Victrola, and a player piano with an antique banjo and mandolin atop. It's difficult to imagine that seven children were raised in such cramped quarters.

Meadow Croft

Cross over a moatlike driveway and enter the wetlands estate called Meadow Croft, the former summer home of John Ellis Roosevelt. First

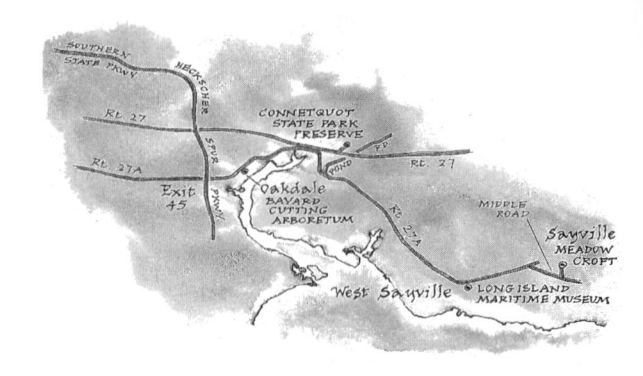

Directions

To Bayard Cutting Arboretum
Southern State Parkway to exit 45 east, which is Route 27A. Go three-quarters of a mile to the arboretum entrance.

To Long Island Maritime Museum
From arboretum, continue east on Route 27A into West Sayville; entrance is on right, just past Suffolk County Golf Course.

To Meadow Croft
From Maritime Museum, take Montauk Highway (Main Street) east through Sayville; just past Railroad Avenue, bear right onto Middle Road. Continue on Middle Road to estate entrance on left.

To Connetquot State Park Preserve
Accessible only from Sunrise Highway going west. Entrance is on right, just west of Pond Road.

---

cousin to Theodore Roosevelt, John Ellis grew up next door to his more famous presidential relative in a townhouse on East 20th Street in Manhattan.

Like his cousin Theodore's family, this branch of the Roosevelt clan was active and athletic. They bicycled, sailed, went motoring in their 1903 Fiat, and golfed on the property. Their swimming pool, only a concrete shell of its former self right now, was reputed to be the first in-ground pool on Long Island, and, in its heydey, was housed within a glass enclosure.

The house itself, painted a cheerful yellow, is a harmonious architectural hybrid put together by architect Isaac Green, who was responsible for many South Shore and Hamptons summer estates. Built during the 1860s by the Woodward family, the house was purchased by Roosevelt in 1890, who had

Green incorporate the original farmhouse into the Colonial Revival design, with its Victorian porches. Currently, the house is being restored to reflect the year 1910. Although it is a work in progress, you can admire the beautiful woodwork in the center hall, with its fine oak staircase and the poplar beams. In the farmhouse section you can view a 15-minute slide show about the Roosevelts. Since the Roosevelt family was actively involved in the art world, John Roosevelt had a workshop in the house (the work bench is the original one) plus a painter's studio in the carriage house.

Upstairs, you can see the progress of the restoration of the bedrooms of Roosevelt's three daughters, done with the assistance of Victoria magazine. Downstairs, is the headquarters of the Bayport Heritage Association, which administers the house, as well as the site of the Robert Roosevelt Nature Library. Outside, stop at the little garden, which has been accurately restored to replicate a kitchen garden of 1910.

An interesting side trip is a visit to the vineyard of Barney Loughlin, a former caretaker of the estate, whose winery is situated in a remote corner of the property. It is not infrequent for Loughlin to hold summer wine tastings. To get to the vineyards, you must travel a dirt road which, in the house's early days, lead to the estate of Roosevelt's brother, Robert Jr., as well as to the home of his father, Robert Sr. Today, Meadow Croft is all that is left of the Roosevelt era in the Sayville-Bayport area.

Connetquot River State Park Preserve (Hiking trails, Southside Sportsman's Club, Trout Hatchery)

Within this most bucolic of parklands, nature-lovers and fitness buffs can enjoy the miles of walking trails. Here, just a few hundred feet from the traffic and bustle of Sunrise Highway, deer graze peacefully, wild turkeys roam and bird-life abounds.

Here, too, is where you can see the Southside Sportsman's Club, a rambling structure that began life in 1820 as Snedeker's Tavern but became the hunting and fishing sanctuary of some of Long Island's foremost millionaires. The stained glass window over the front door was, not surprisingly, done by club member Louis Comfort Tiffany. You'll pass through rooms full of old lockers, the separate men's and ladies' dining rooms, a stuffed bird exhibit, an environmentally themed gift shop, and a habitat exhibit whose showcases tell the story of the wildlife present in Long Island's state park environments — the North Shore forests,

Newsday Photo / Don Jacobsen
The dining room at the mansion at Bayard Cutting Arboretum

pine barrens, freshwater wetlands and salt marshes. A children's touch tank is filled with things one might find on a beach. There's also a collection of bird's eggs. Look out the window, and you'll see the William Nicoll gristmill, which has been on the property since the 1750s.

Up the road about a mile is the Trout Hatchery, which dates back to 1890 and claims to be the oldest fish hatchery on Long Island. Fed by the Connetquot River, which comes down a canal, the facility hatches brook trout, brown trout and rainbow trout. Children will delight in feeding the fish food from a dispenser and watching the trout jump. Indoors, you'll see the eggs themselves, which are kept in trays within the hatchery troughs. The trout, raised for fly-fishing programs on Long Island waters, take about eight weeks to hatch.

Important Information

Bayard Cutting Arboretum
Montauk Highway
Oakdale
516-581-1002

Open: Year-round, Wednesday to Sunday and legal holidays, 10 a.m. to sunset
Fee: $4 per vehicle (early April to Labor Day, then weekends only till end of October)
Tours: Group tours by reservation only; call in advance

Rest rooms: Yes
On-site food: Seasonal on-site snack bar, Tuesday to Sunday, 11:30 a.m. to 4 p.m., early April to Labor Day, and weekends till end of October
Wheelchair access: Yes
Gift shop: Saturday, Sunday, Wednesday, 1 p.m. to 4 p.m.
Child appropriate: Yes

Long Island Maritime Museum
86 West Ave.
West Sayville
516-854-4974

Open: Wednesday to Saturday, 10 a.m. to 3 p.m., Sunday, noon to 4 p.m.; other times by appointment.
Fee: Suggested donation $3, $1.50 children, free to museum members
Tours: Available by appointment
Rest rooms: Yes
On-site food: No
Wheelchair access: Yes
Gift shop: Yes
Child appropriate: Yes

Meadow Croft
Middle Road
Sayville
516-854-4970

Open: Hours: Late June to late October; Sunday only, noon to 5 p.m.; formal tours given at 1 p.m. and 3 p.m. (same hours for vineyard)
Fee: Donation to Bayport Heritage Association toward restoration is appreciated
Tours: Yes; formal tours given at 1 p.m. and 3 p.m.
Rest rooms: Yes
On-site food: Picnic area on site
Wheelchair access: Yes (first floor only)
Gift shop: Souvenir items for sale by Bayport Heritage Association
Child appropriate: Older children

Connetquot State Park Preserve
Sunrise Highway
Oakdale
516-581-1005

Open: Hours: Daily, 8 a.m. to 4:30 p.m.
Fee: Vehicle use fee of $4
Tours: Call environmental office at 516-581-1072.
Rest rooms: Administration building and hatchery
On-site food: No
Wheelchair access: Yes
Gift shop: Yes
Child-appropriate: Yes

Where to Eat

Savory Fare and Desserts
59-61 Main St.
Sayville
567-8382
At this charming little cafe-within-a-bakery, the chef executes an imaginative, flavor-intense menu of homestyle favorites. Clam chowder served in a sourdough bread bowl is a must, and substantial enough to qualify as bargain a midday meal. Dinner entrees are a little pricier, but well worth it.

Cafe Joelle
25 Main St.
Sayville
589-4600
One of Sayville's most popular spots, this small but sophisticated cafe offers a creative contemporary American menu in warm, unpretentious surroundings. If you're planning on dinner, it pays to call ahead, since weekends can be especially hectic here.

Aegean Cafe
35 Main St.
Sayville
589-5529
At this friendly little Greek taverna, they feed you well and — if you're on a tight schedule — they get you out on time. Sandwiches — either the veal or chicken souvlaki — are savory standouts. You won't find anything out of the ordinary, mind you, but everything is fresh, lively, and satisfying. The prices are nice, too.

OLD BETHPAGE VILLAGE RESTORATION

You could call it The Village That Time Forgot or you could think of it as The Village That Remembers When. Here, within a bucolic setting made up of over 55 historic structures, the past springs vividly to life as "villagers" in period costume enthusiastically reenact the roles of 19th Century craftspeople, tradesfolk and farmers.

In a sense, Old Bethpage Village Restoration may accurately be termed The Village that Never Was, since each of its buildings originated somewhere else on Long Island.

Keep in mind that while most of the interior furnishings you see may not be site-original, the majority are period pieces that closely replicate what was. You may be wondering why this is the only one-stop tour in this book.

That's because there's just so much to see and do within one area. What's important, too, is that you don't feel rushed.

Perhaps the Restoration's newsletter, the Old Bethpage Enquirer, says it best: "Slow down. Enter a peaceful world . . . Try to imagine yourself living in this environment. Stroll around the village at a leisurely pace, talk to the villagers, and let new and unfamiliar sensations penetrate your consciousness."

Newsday Photo / Bill Davis

A game of base ball played with 1887 rules and uniforms

The time-transition begins at the reception center, where you can pick up a map of the area as well as literature to assist you on your self-guided tour. Remember, at nearly every site you'll meet staff-members eager to provide added insights and answer any questions you might have.

The oldest house in the restoration (also believed to be the oldest surviving Dutch house in Nassau County) is the Schenck farmhouse from Manhasset, which was built in 1730 by brothers Minne and Roeloff Schenk, now restored to the year 1765. Here, the parlor, used for entertaining, includes, among its furnishings, a bed. This was customary in many pre-Revolutionary Dutch homes, a way for a prosperous family to impress their guests with fine bed linens. The sitting / dining room, although equipped with a hearth, was not used as a kitchen. Meals were cooked in the slave quarters and brought to the main house.

Perhaps the most charming feature of this house, though, is the bedbox, a snug little bed built, cupboardlike, into the wall, to help avoid the cold from the drafty walls. In the house, you'll also see a classic Dutch wardrobe known as a kas and a cozy girls' bedroom with a table invitingly set for tea. An interesting bit of trivia: the Schenck House was broken into and robbed twice, once by forces loyal to the British, and another time by a band of all-American petty thieves.

The Conklin House, relocated from the Village

of the Branch, is a small Cape Cod-style bayman's home, belonging to Joseph (Hull) Conklin, and restored to reflect the year 1853, when the Conklins' only child was quite young. Consequently, you'll see a 19th-Century baby-tender (a forerunner of the high chair) and an antique potty chair. In Conklin's workroom, there are some examples of the craft of net-making. A little side-note: Walt Whitman, it is believed, boarded here as a young man, while teaching school in the Village of the Branch.

Every village had its general store. At the circa 1866 Layton Store originally of East Norwich, men played checkers on top of an old barrel, warmed by a wood burning stove. The store's wooden shelves are stocked with all manner of items: spices, tobacco, dolls, patent medicines, irons, dry goods, gunpowder, toys and spectacles. The pottery you see is from the famous Brown Brothers pottery works in Huntington. There's also an early version of a washing machine. Go through the back door, and you'll enter the Layton House, which is attached to the store. The kitchen, modern for its day, is filled with advances that represented some degree of freedom from the drudgery of the era: indoor plumbing, an ice-box and a wood-burning cookstove.

On the grounds, you'll pass the Bach Blacksmith Shop from Hicksville, restored to 1875, and the Luyster Store from East Norwich, restored to 1850; here, Theodore Roosevelt is reputed to have shopped. Visit the working hat shop, once owned by Louis Ritch of Middle Island, which has been restored to the year 1830.

Then, there's the Hempstead home of Peter Cooper, the inventor, industrialist, founder of the Cooper Union Institute in Manhattan, and presidential candidate. The original section of the house was built during the late 1600s, but what you see reflects the year 1815, when Cooper, a newlywed and fledgling inventor, lived there. Inside, you'll see a warm, homey sitting room, dining room, parlor, and back bedroom. A workroom, equipped with a loom, is used for weaving demonstrations.

While walking down the dirt road leading to the Powell Farm — the only restored property original to this site — you'll pass a fenced-in pasture, the frequent grazing haunt of Lynette, one of a rare breed of Lineback cows. By the barn, you may want to stop to see Mick and Bud, the two sweet-tempered Devon oxen who are part of the farm family. There also are two pigs, named — yes, really — Al and Tipper. Because the actual Powell barn was in such poor condition, the barn you see was transported from the Underhill property in Syosset. Photographs indicate that it was nearly identical to the original, and not by mere coincidence, since the Powells and the

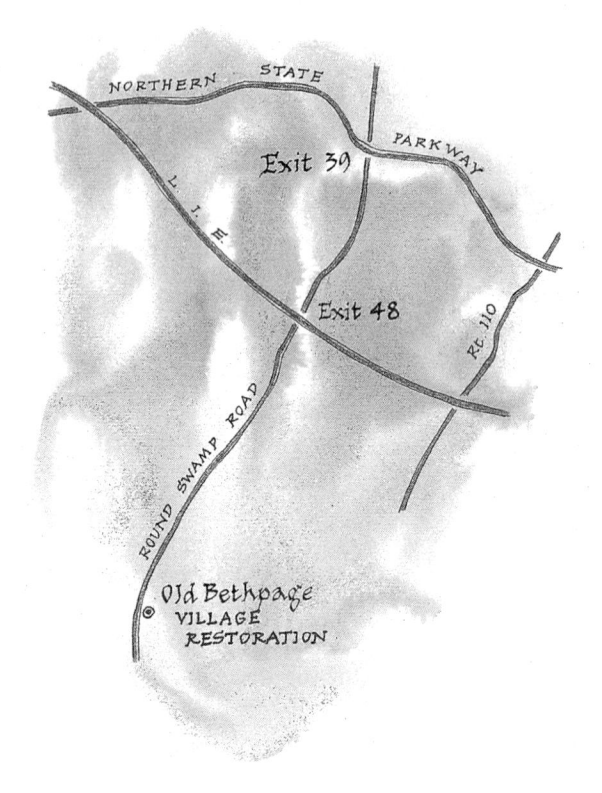

Directions

To Old Bethpage Village Restoration
Long Island Expressway to exit 48 south; or Northern State Parkway to exit 39 south (Round Swamp Road); continue on Round Swamp Road, following signs to Restoration entrance.

Underhills were related. The Powell farmhouse, which mirrored the year 1855, was damaged by a recent fire and will re-open to the public soon.

Unlike most of the properties here, the Williams farmhouse, originally located in New Hyde Park and restored to the year 1860, has many of its original furnishings. In the formal parlor, the wine-colored Empire sofa was a Williams piece, as was the silk embroidered memorial over the mantle. The Dutch kas in the bedroom, as well as the bed itself may be counted among the originals, as well.

The little Greek Revival Kirby House from Hempstead, restored to the year 1845, belonged to a tailor named Richard Kirby. The dining room, which also doubled as a sitting room, is a comfortable-looking contrast to the rather stiff, formal parlor.

Kirby was a member of the Hempstead Light Guards, a militia unit from which he received many a tailoring job; you can see Kirby's militia coat in the little tailor shop in back of the house. But Kirby was a man with loftier ambitions than sewing clothes and, in 1846, he was ordained a Methodist minister. As you leave the house, walk around to the back, where you'll find a grape arbor and a little garden.

You must be quiet as a mouse when entering the District No. 6 School House, an 1845 one-room school from Manhasset, since, frequently, class is in session. Take a seat and learn a few lessons from a 19th-Century textbook; perhaps you'll get an opportunity to write on an old-fashioned slate. While you're here, take note of the graduated size of desks, with the smaller ones in front for the younger students and the larger ones toward the back.

The 1857 Manetto Hill Methodist Church is a site often used for after-hours weddings. It's a Greek Revival building that's stark, simple and utilitarian in design.

If you want to hoist a few at the local tavern, the circa 1850 Noon Inn will be able to provide you with liquid refreshment, although nothing stronger than an old-fashioned root beer. Originally located in East Meadow, this inn, unlike most from that period, was built specifically to function as a tavern. Downstairs is the bar room, with a private kitchen and parlor next door. Upstairs, you can see the living quarters where innkeepers John and Mary Ann Noon had a bedroom next door to the room kept for Mary Ann's sister. You'll also find a guest room, and a public ballroom sometimes used for the Restoration's special occasions.

There are, of course, more sites than the ones outlined here. Remember that at any given time, some buildings are undergoing repair and are not open to the public.

Before you leave, keep in mind that the Restoration offers a host of educational programs and special events; be sure to pick up current listings. The staff has even gone so far as to organize two 19th-Century base ball (that's how they used to spell it) leagues. Rules and uniforms are true-to-period. Time-tripping, for some, can well become a way of life.

Important Information

Old Bethpage Village Restoration
Round Swamp Road
Old Bethpage
516-572-8400

Open: March through October, Wednesday to

Sunday, 10 a.m. to 5 p.m., November and December, 10 a.m. to 4 p.m.; January and February, closed. Open Memorial Day, July 4th, Labor Day, and Columbus Day; closed all other holidays.
Fee: $6 adults; $4 children and seniors.
Tours: At additional fee, by appointment only.
Rest rooms: Yes
On-site food: On-site cafeteria in season
Wheelchair access: Some areas
Gift shop: Yes.
Child appropriate: Yes

Where to Eat

Maxia
560 Steward Ave.
Bethpage
516-942-0776
This highly polished Vietnamese gem offers vibrant and well-priced fare in friendly, unhurried surroundings. Soups are truly wonderful, and they do some amazing things with salmon.

Yamato
1115 Old Country Rd.
Plainview
516-433-3277
For a relaxing break from a morning (or afternoon) on your feet, ask to be seated in one of the private tatami rooms at this inviting Japanese restaurant. Both the sushi and the cooked fare are highly recommended. Lunch is offered only on weekdays.

West Coast Kitchen
377-2 S. Oyster Bay Rd.
Plainview
516-931-8300
You can get all manner of wraps at this informal little order-at-the-counter eatery tucked away in a little niche of the Plainview shopping center. These quick, hand-held, easy-to-eat rolled sandwiches are both creative and flavorsome. They've also got a long list of healthful "smoothie" drinks, many of them made with fresh fruit.

THE DRIVE-BY ARCHITECTURAL TOURS

Architecture, because of its functional nature, is an art form we often overlook. We see a bank as a place to transact business, a school as a seat of learning, a church or synagogue as a house of worship. And, while we're not incorrect, we often miss out on the intrinsic beauty and historical significance of these useful buildings.

So, let's open our eyes and go for a ride. We've planned this architectural tour in two loops, one in Nassau, the other in Western Suffolk, each navigable in a day.

For anyone wishing further guidance, or wishing to add an architectural jaunt to any of the four East End tours, check out the AIA Architectural Guide to Nassau and Suffolk Counties, put out by the American Institute of Architects, Long Island Chapter, and The Society for the Preservation of Long Island Antiquities, an invaluable source in planning this tour.

Directions follow each destination. Happy motoring!

Loop 1 — Nassau

St. Agnes Cathedral

We begin in Rockville Centre at the imposing Norman Gothic St. Agnes Cathedral, a light-colored brick edifice which serves as headquarters of the Roman Catholic Diocese of Rockville Centre. The parish began by celebrating its first mass in an 1887 blacksmith shop on Centre Avenue; today, on the front and side of the cathedral, an anvil commemorates that mass. As the parish grew, a small marble church was built in 1905. You may see some of the marble from that church in stonework around the campus, in particular some of the driveway entrances. In 1933, Msgr. Philip Quealy, pastor-administrator for the church from the early 1900s to the 1950s, decided to build the grand building we see today.

Take Sunrise Highway (Route 27) to North Park Avenue in Rockville Centre and turn north. Proceed to College Place, directly north of the Long Island Rail Road station, and turn left. St. Agnes is on the corner of College Place and Clinton Avenue.

The Brooklyn Waterworks

The Brooklyn Waterworks (once known as the Milburn Pumping Station) in Freeport lies in majestic ruins. Once one of the most beautiful utilitarian works of architecture on Long Island, it was built during the 1890s, according to a design by architect Frank Freeman of Brooklyn, in the Romanesque revival style of architect H.H. Richardson. Note the graceful archways and intricate brickwork. The complex is under restoration by a developer and may be converted into a nursing facility.

To reach it from the cathedral, return in the direction you came from along College Place to North Park Avenue, turn right and then left onto Sunrise Highway; continue on Sunrise through Baldwin to Freeport, turn left at Brookside Avenue; the Waterworks will be on your left, north of the railroad tracks.

The Long Beach Station House

With its graceful arches and red-tiled roof, the Spanish-style Long Beach station house is a reminder of that city's glory days as a seaside resort. It was constructed in 1909, according to a design by architect Kenneth M. Murchison, who also designed Union Railroad Station in Baltimore. In 1986, equipped with a $2.3 million federal grant and a 1914 photograph, the City of Long Beach restored the station to its original appearance.

From Brookside Avenue, turn right onto Sunrise Highway, heading back west to Long Beach Road in Rockville Centre, where you turn left. Proceed through Oceanside, bearing left at fork to Austin Boulevard and crossing bridge into Long Beach (the street you are on will be called Long Beach Boulevard again); turn right at West Park Avenue and continue to LIRR station, on your right.

The Lido Beach Hotel

Breathtaking is the word that best describes the

Lido Beach Hotel, an enormous 1928 Spanish Renaissance castle with a red tiled roof and fanciful minarets. It was designed by Schultze & Weaver, the architectural firm that also did the Waldorf Astoria in Manhattan and the Montauk Manor on the East End. During the heyday of Long Beach's development as a major resort, the hotel boasted an 18-hole golf course and a ballroom with a retractable roof. Today, it's a condominium, and can be viewed only from behind gates.

To go from the LIRR station's parking lot turn left onto West Park Avenue; proceed east, turning right onto Maple Boulevard and then left onto Richmond Road.

The Jones Beach Water Tower

When Robert Moses comissioned Jones Beach's 231-foot high Water Tower, it was with the free-standing bell tower (campanile) in Venice's St. Marks Square in mind. Moses saw the regal obelisk as symbolic of all his lofty aspirations for this vast public playground as well as the parkways leading to and from the beach. Symbolism aside, the tower also has a practical purpose, since instead of housing a bell, it holds a large metal tank where water, drawn from deep wells, is stored for the entire park facility.

Return from the hotel via Maple Boulevard to West Park Avenue, now called Lido Boulevard, and turn right, proceeding to Loop Parkway, where you turn left. Follow signs to Meadowbrook Parkway south to Jones Beach; on Ocean Parkway, follow signs to West Bath House.

EAB Plaza

Sleek, sculptural, and shimmering, the two 15-story EAB Plaza buildings dominate the landscape. Designed by the Spector Group in 1984, this stunning contemporary work of architecture features an indoor atrium complete with tropical foliage and a fountain, which converts to an ice-skating rink in winter. At Christmas the plaza is the site of a stunning tree-lighting, with a tree that's even bigger than the one at Rockefeller Center.

From the beach return to Ocean Parkway, following the signs to the Meadowbrook Parkway. Go north on the Meadowbrook to exit M5, Route 24 west. Immediately on your left, you will see EAB Plaza.

St. Paul's School

Surely one of the most magnificent edifices on Long Island, St. Paul's School was built in 1879 as part of the legacy of regal buildings Cornelia Stewart built in memory of her husband, Garden City founder Alexander Stewart. It's hard not to be awed by this dark red brick chateau-style Gothic piece, complete with intricate iron work and a mansard

The St. Paul's School, which was built in 1879 in Garden City
Newsday Photo / Alan Raia

roof. The school will shortly be converted into an assisted living center, and its historical integrity will be preserved during the renovation.

From EAB, continue west on Hempstead Turnpike to Cathedral Avenue; turn right on Cathedral and proceed to intersection of Cherry Valley and Stewart Avenues; turn left onto Stewart; school is on right.

Country Life Press

Although the Tudor Revival building you see is in a state of near-decay, its grandeur is still apparent. Once the home of Doubleday Page and Company, it was designed by the firm of Kirby & Petit and erected in 1910. It was beautifully landscaped and housed both offices and printing facilities in one building. You'll be struck by the un-industrial appearance of the plant, which looks more like a prep school than a major publishing operation that, in its day, had its own stop on the Long Island Rail Road. Doubleday has repurchased the property and its use has yet to be decided.

Reverse your direction on Stewart Avenue and then make a sharp right onto Cathedral Avenue, passing the Cathedral of the Incarnation [see Hempstead-Garden City tour]. Turn left at Seventh Street and then right at Franklin Avenue; proceed about a block to Country Life Press on the left.

The Nassau County Courthouse

Designed by architect William Bunker Tubby, the Nassau County Courthouse, with its lovely burnished dome, was done in the Renaissance Revival style. Any resemblance to the nation's Capitol in Washington, D.C., was purely intentional.

Reverse direction on Franklin Avenue, heading north. Just before Old Country Road, you'll see the Nassau County Courthouse on your left.

The Roslyn Clock Tower

Perhaps the most famous landmark in the village of Roslyn is the wonderful stone-block Ellen E. Ward Memorial Clock Tower, built in honor of an active community member who died in 1893. It was designed by the firm of Lamb & Rich in New York, who also designed Sagamore Hill in Oyster Bay. The tower's bell, which weighs about 2,500 pounds, was originally used as a fire alarm. Today, it tolls on special occasions. Look at the massive stone blocks and at the tower's Gothic details; both are characteristic of the style of architect Henry Hobson Richardson, who helped establish the Romanesque Revival style of Victorian architecture.

From Franklin, turn right on Old Country Road and then left on Roslyn Road, proceeding north through East Williston all the way into Roslyn, to the clock tower.

Nassau County Museum of Art

This glorious museum (actually worth a major stop) was once the Bryce-Frick Estate known as Clayton. Designed in the neo-Georgian style by architect Ogden Codeman Jr. in 1895, it was built for New York State Paymaster-General Lloyd Bryce. In 1917, it was bought by Childs Frick, son of Henry Clay Frick, who helped found the Carnegie Steel Corp. Take time to admire both the mansion and the trellis in its garden, a lovely and unusual work of landscape architecture.

Turn right onto Old Northern Boulevard to Broadway, turn right onto entry ramp for Northern Boulevard; continue east until you see a sign for the museum on your left; turn left into museum.

Trinity Episcopal Church

Quietly elegant, the Stanford White-designed Trinity Episcopal Church was built in the Norman-Early English Revival style. You might want to go inside and view the magnificent stained glass windows, which include two Tiffany pieces. The church was put on the National Register of Historic Places in 1986.

Return to Northern Boulevard, turning right and heading west to the intersection of Church Street, turn right to view the Trinity Episcopal Church on the corner.

The Village of Sea Cliff

This charming community is, in effect, a living Victorian museum of architecture. Drive up and down some of the winding lanes and you'll find countless colorful examples of the Carpenter Gothic style, a style so-named because it used wood and paint to emulate the stone details of the homes of the very affluent. For a detailed walking tour, you might want to stop into the Sea Cliff Village Museum, 95 10th Ave., 516-671-0090. Try to to see the Woodshed on Central Avenue

Newsday Photo / Bill Davis

The Wetherhill House in St. James, designed by Stanford White

off Sea Cliff Avenue, a rainbow-hued 1890s marvel that perhaps best exemplifies the free-wheeling Victorian spirit of the area. It is a private home, so be careful not to disturb its inhabitants.

To get to the village proceed north on Church Street to Summit Avenue, turn left, and turn right onto Bryant Avenue; follow Bryant Avenue until the road forks, then take Glenwood Road toward the left. Go to Scudders Lane and turn left and then right on Shore Road, which becomes Prospect Avenue. Proceed on Prospect, turning right to Sea Cliff Avenue.

Suffolk County - Loop 2

Coindre Hall

We'll start our Suffolk tour at Coindre Hall, a magnificent chateaulike estate with rounded towers and a French Gothic facade. Formerly known as West Neck Farm, this 1910 house was designed for industrialist McKesson Brown by architect Clarence Luce. After Brown lost the house in the stock market crash of 1929, the estate became a Catholic School called Coindre Hall. Currently, it's owned by the Suffolk County Department of Parks, which is restoring parts of it to its estate days; still, sections added by the school will remain. To be called the Long Island Gold Coast Museum, it will feature comprehensive exhibits on those fabulous mansions from those fabulous days.

Long Island Expressway to exit 49 north (Route 110). Take Route 110 past the center of Huntington, where it is called New York Avenue, continuing north to Mill Dam Road, turn left. Then proceed to West Shore Road, and turn right. Coindre Hall is at the point where West Shore turns into Brown.

Huntington Village

Two of Huntington's finest landmark buildings were the work of architectural firm Cady, Berg & See, who also did a wing of the American Museum of Natural History in Manhattan. The strikingly handsome Tudor Revival Soldiers and Sailors Memorial Building was erected in 1892 as a symbol of the town's patriotism and pride. It is now the town historian's office. Across the street, at 209 Main St., is another Tudor Revival building, the Huntington Sewing and Trade School which opened in 1900 and today functions as the home of the Huntington Historical Society.

Back-track to New York Avenue and proceeding south to Route 25A (Main Street), where you turn left. The Huntington Sewing and Trade School Building is one block on your left, Soldiers and Sailors Monument across the street.

Northport Village

In terms of architecture, the village of Northport is, at least architecturally, snugly ensconced in the 19th Century. Before cruising down Main Street, whose facades reflect that bygone era, you might want to explore the waterfront park, with its dock and nostalgic-looking gazebo. On Main Street, stop into the 1914 Andrew Carnegie library building, home of the Northport Historical Society, to pick up two brochures, one detailing the individual histories of the stores along Main Street and the other identifying the Victorian houses along Bayview Avenue, many of them former sea captains' homes.

Continue east from Huntington on Route 25A past Centerport; left onto Woodbine Avenue; right onto Main Street.

The Wetherhill House

The lovely countryside around St. James was home to world-renowned architect Stanford White. Here, on a bluff overlooking Stony Brook Harbor, is the grand shingled and gabled octagonal Wetherill House, which White designed for his sister-in-law Kate Smith Wetherill. Remember: this is a private dwelling, so you don't want to be intrusive.

Continue east on Main Street to Route 25A; turn left on 25A and continue through Kings Park and Smithtown (watch the signs because the road turns twice) into St. James. Go north on Moriches Road; right onto Three Sisters Road and quick left onto Harbor Hill Road.

St. James Station House

An absolute must-see in St. James is the Victorian

beige-white-and-green station house with its whimsical gingerbread trim. Built in 1873, it is the Long Island Railroad's oldest operating station house and is listed on the National Register of Historic Places. It was rebuilt to mint condition in 1997, all in accordance with provisions of the National Historic Preservation Act. The woodburning potbellied stove you see is the original and has been reconditioned but is not operating.

Backtrack to Moriches Road, turning left onto Route 25A passing St. James Episcopal Church. At Lake Avenue turn right; go to the station on your left.

North Shore Jewish Center

Built in 1975 according to a design by the firm Landow & Landow, the quietly dramatic North Shore Jewish Center was the recipient of the AIA Long Island Chapter's Archi Award, given to outstanding works of Long Island community architecture. The long, low building features a front that seems to soar upward, like the prow of a ship. Note that the center is also is one of Long Island's oldest Jewish congregations, established in 1896.

From Lake Avenue, turn right onto Route 25A, continue east through Stony Brook, turn right onto Bennetts Road; then left onto Lower Sheep Pasture Road; continue to intersection of Old Town Road and turn right; the center will be shortly on your left, across from Ward Melville High School.

Idle Hour

This is the former William K. Vanderbilt estate, which now functions as the campus of Dowling College. The house you see, however, is not the original one that Vanderbilt commissioned architect Richard Morris Hunt to build in 1876; that home was destroyed by a fire in 1899. Shortly afterwards, Hunt's son, Richard Howland Hunt (famous for having completed his father's design for the Metropolitan Museum of Art) drew up the plans for this house, which incorporates Flemish and Renaissance European styles of architecture. Among the estate's subsequent owners was mobster Dutch Schultz.

From North Shore Jewish Center: Left out of parking lot, continue to Boyle Road, turn right on Boyle Road to Middle Country Road (Route 25), turn left, then almost immediately right, onto College Road; turn right at Mooney Pond Road, right onto Horse Block Lane, and left onto Nicolls Road; proceed on Nicolls Road all the way south to Montauk Highway (Route 27A), turn right, heading west. Proceed through Bayport and Sayville to Oakdale; turn left at Idle Hour Boulevard, following signs to Dowling College.

St. Mark's Episcopal Church

Although a headline-making fire in 1989 seriously

damaged St. Mark's Episcopal Church in Islip, that architecturally magnificent 1880 house of worship has since been restored. Built by William K. Vanderbilt, this Scandinavian Timberwork church was designed by Richard Morris Hunt, one of the premier architects of the day. Note the complex roof angles, the fanciful Nordic gargoyles, the lovely stained-glass windows, among them a Tiffany creation. The quintessential country church, St. Mark's included among its parishioners several Vanderbilts as well as William Bayard Cutting. The parish house on the property was designed by prominent architect Isaac H. Green.

From Idle Hour Boulevard, turn left onto Montauk Highway; proceed west to Islip; St. Marks church will be on your left, at Route 111.

St. Patrick's Roman Catholic Church

While Bay Shore's Main Street has undergone many economic changes, a reassuring landmark continues to be the lovely Romanesque St. Patrick's Roman Catholic Church, designed by Manhattan architect Gustave E. Steinbeck in 1919. The brickwork and mosaic are worthy of admiration, as is the beautiful octagonal dome.

Proceed on Montauk Highway to community of Bay Shore; St. Patrick's church will be on right at intersection of Fifth Avenue.

Aluminaire House

The tiny, boxy Aluminaire House in Central Islip was designed by architects Kocher & Frey as a prototype to be exhibited at the Architectural and Allied Arts Exposition in New York City during the early 1930s. Quite a curiosity, it was covered entirely with aluminum panels and made up of parts that could be screwed together. Currently, it's undergoing restoration and should soon be its old shiny self.

On Fifth Avenue, proceed north to Route 27, Sunrise Highway, head east to Carleton Avenue; go north on Carleton to New York Institute of Technology Campus, whose entrance is on your right; on campus, turn left at the church and continue along road; the Aluminaire house will be on your right.

ONE-STOP DESTINATIONS

Here are a few spots that are really worth seeing even though they didn't fit neatly into the other tours we've planned. These outings can fill an afternoon or be tacked onto other tours, if you're in the neighborhood.

Hicksville Gregory Museum
Hicksville

This little museum, housed in a building once used as a courthouse, boasts a fine collection of rocks, minerals, and fossils. But you'll probably want to focus on the preserved turn-of-the-century jail cell in the rear of the museum. Dating to 1915, the cell, which was used as a holding facility for local offenders waiting to be transferred to the county jail, boasts a bunk bed filled by two life-sized dummy prisoners, a toilet that doesn't flush, and a cold water sink. Outside, there's a solid steel door with a window, which attending officers would look out of when the paddy wagon pulled up. The jail, which only housed small-time crooks, closed in 1937.

Van Nostrand-Starkins House
Roslyn

This little cottage tucked away in Roslyn is actually the oldest surviving building in Nassau County. It was built around 1680 by a family named Van Nostrand about whom not much is actually known. The house was acquired by a blacksmith named Starkins during the 18th Century and has been restored to reflect that period.

William Floyd Estate
Mastic Beach

William Floyd, Long Island's only signer of the Declaration of Independence, was born at this Mastic plantation in 1734. During the Revolutionary War, while he was in Philadelphia, his

William Floyd's traveling case for his sherry, on display at the Floyd Estate.

Newsday Photo / Bill Davis

wife and children were forced to flee to Connecticut. While the Floyds were gone, it is believed that the house was plundered and so, upon his return in 1783, William set about restoring much of what was damaged and adding an extension. At age 69, he moved to Utica. He died there at age 86. But the house continued to be occupied by members of the Floyd family long afterward.

What's fascinating about the Floyd estate, which was built incrementally beginning in 1724, is that it shows the continuation of one family's life for about 260 years. Your tour guide will take you through a veritable warren of rooms and wings, some of which seem tacked on as afterthoughts. You'll see, in just one room, an 18th-Century Windsor chair, a 19th-Century sideboard, and a 1950 drum table, all Floyd family heirlooms. By the way, the Peale portrait of William Floyd on display here is a copy of the original, which hangs in Philadelphia.

Afterwards, you might want to explore the outbuildings — a carriage barn, an ice house, and a blacksmith shop — or ramble about the 613-acre property on 8.5 miles of walking trails.

Old Halsey House
Southampton

There's talk that the Old Halsey House in Southampton is haunted. As the story goes, the house (believed to be the oldest English frame house in New York State) was built in 1648 by Thomas Halsey, whose wife was murdered the next year.

Whether or not you'll encounter Mrs. Halsey's ghost is questionable, but what you will find is a wonderful old home that's been restored to its 17th-

Newsday Photo / Don Jacobsen
The symbol of the East End: The Big Duck in Flanders

Century appearance by the Southampton Colonial Society.

While what you see may not be the original Halsey furnishings, the pieces are authentic to their period. Note that all the fireplaces in the house are at the center and connected to one chimney. Leaded glass windows were copied from one of the surviving originals.

Outside, an herb garden with an English border has been lovingly maintained by the Olde Towne Garden club. Think of adding this spot to the East Hampton or Sag Harbor tour.

And while you're at it, ask about the Colonial Society's walking tours of the area.

The Big Duck
Flanders

What's 20 feet high, weighs 10 tons, looks like a duck but doesn't walk like a duck? It's the Big Duck, a proud Long Island landmark and an example of roadside architecture.

The Big Duck was born during 1930s as a Riverhead farm stand, back when the East End was duck-farming country.

Moved in 1988 to its present site in Flanders, on Route 24, the duck houses within its body the Big Duck Museum shop, offering a variety of duck-themed items for sale and is open from Memorial Day to Labor Day.

Northport Historical Society
Northport

The charming brick Tudor-style edifice belonging to the Northport Historical Society began life in 1914 as a library, built with a gift from Andrew Carnegie, who helped build libraries all over the country. Today, the museum houses a permanent collection of memorabilia and photographs outlining Northport's past as well as a series of changing exhibits on the area.

The architecturally striking main room is dominated by a reproduction of the mast of a 19th-Century ship, the Allie R. Chester. As part of the permanent exhibit, which rims the room, you'll see a chair from 1758, an ornamental box that was a relic of the War of 1812, and an 1820 marquetry ship's carpenters' chest. There are some marvelous archival photographs of Northport's Main Street as well as a 1903 diorama of that thoroughfare located downstairs, in another exhibit room. Worth seeking out is the painting made during the 1890s by local artist Jim Ackerley that depicts an Asharoken hunting party.

Before you leave, pick up a brochure outlining a walking tour of the Main Street area.

Important Information

Hicksville Gregory Museum
Heitz Place and Bay Avenue
Hicksville
516-822-7505

Directions: Long Island Expressway to exit 41 south (Route 106 / 107); turn left at Bethpage Road, take right fork to Oyster Bay Road; follow signs to museum at Heitz Place and Bay Avenue
Open: Year-round (closed major holidays) Tuesday to Friday, 9:30 a.m. to 4:30 p.m., Saturday and Sunday, 1 p.m. to 5 p.m.
Fee: $3 adults, $1.50 children over 6 and senior citizens.
Tours: Groups only
Rest rooms: Yes
On-site food: No
Wheelchair access: First floor only
Gift shop: Yes
Child appropriate: Older children

Van Nostrand-Starkins House
221 Main St.
Roslyn
516-621-2153

Directions: Long Island Expressway to exit 37 south (Mineola Avenue); take south service road to Roslyn Road, turn right, heading north; it becomes Main Street in Roslyn; house is on right.
Open: June to late October, Tuesday, Wednesday, Thursday, Saturday and Sunday, 1 p.m. to 4 p.m.
Fee: $1
Tours: Informal
Rest rooms: No
On-site food: No
Wheelchair access: No
Gift shop: No
Child appropriate: Older children.

William Floyd Estate
245 Park Ave.
Mastic Beach
516-399-2030

Directions: Long Island Expressway to exit 68 south, William Floyd Parkway; drive about four miles, crossing Montauk Highway to Haven Wood Drive, Mastic Beach; left at traffic light onto Haven Wood, which merges into Neighborhood Road, which you take through town of Mastic Beach to end. Turn left onto Park Drive, continue to Visitor Entrance Gate, which will be on right
Open: Memorial Day to Labor Day, Friday to Sunday and holiday Mondays, 11 a.m. to 5 p.m.
Fee: Free (donations accepted)
Tours: Yes, usually every half-hour
Rest rooms: Port-a-lavs only
On-site food: No
Wheelchair access: Information unavailable
Gift shop: No
Child-appropriate: Older children.

Old Halsey House
South Main Street
Southampton
516-283-2494

Directions: Sunrise Highway; right at North Sea Road, which becomes Main Street; follow south and house is a half-mile south of the intersection of Job's Lane and Main Street, on right.
Open: June 12 to September 15, Tuesday to Sunday (closed Mondays), 11 a.m. to 5 p.m.
Fee: $2 adults, $.50 children
Tours: Informal
Rest rooms: No
On-site food: No

Wheelchair access: No
Gift shop: No
Child-appropriate: Older children

Big Duck
Route 24
Flanders Rd.
Flanders (Southampton)
516-852-8292

Directions: From Sunrise Highway, take Route 24 north to Flanders; from Riverhead, follow Route 24 south
Open: Seasonal, call for hours
Fee: Free
Tours: No
Rest rooms: Information unavailable
On-site food: No
Wheelchair access: Yes
Gift shop: Yes
Child appropriate: Yes

Northport Historical Society Museum
215 Main St.
Northport
516-757-9859

Directions: Long Island Expressway to exit 52 north or Northern State exit 42 north (Route 231); stay right onto Deer Park Road, which joins Jericho Turnpike (Route 25). Immediately get into left turning lane and make left at first light onto Elwood Road. Proceed on Elwood crossing Route 25A, where street becomes Reservoir Avenue; continue on Reservoir, which becomes Church Street. Turn left at Main Street; continue to Historical Society on right
Open: Year round, Tuesday to Sunday, 1 p.m. to 4:30 p.m.
Fee: Suggested donation $2
Tours: Available by appointment
Rest rooms: Yes
On-site food: No
Wheelchair access: No
Gift shop: Yes
Child appropriate: Yes

THE WINERIES OF LONG ISLAND

Ranking right up there, with the vintages of California and the Pacific Northwest, the wines of Long Island's East End have garnered praise and recognition nationwide as well as abroad. Visit the many wineries, taste and marvel at the variety and quality of vintages and find out just what kind of magic it takes to turn grapes into wine.

Bedell Cellars, Cutchogue. 734-7537
Bidwell Vineyards, Cutchogue. 734-5200
Channing Daughters, Bridgehampton. 537-7224
Corey Creek Vineyards, Southold. 765-4168
Duck Walk Vineyards, Water Mill. 726-7555
Gristina Vineyards, Cutchogue. 734-7089
Hargrave Vineyard, Cutchogue. 734-5111
Jamesport Vineyards, Jamesport. 722-5256
Laurel Lake Vineyards, Laurel. 298-1420
Lenz Winery, Peconic. 734-6010
Macari Vineyards, Mattituck. 298-0100
Osprey's Dominion Vineyards, Peconic. 765-6188
Palmer Vineyards, Aquebogue. 722-9463
Paumanok Vineyards, Aquebogue. 722-8800
Peconic Bay Vineyards, Cutchogue. 734-7361
Pellegrini Vineyards, Cutchogue. 734-4111
Pindar Vineyards, Peconic. 734-6200
Pugliese Vineyards, Cutchogue. 734-4057
Sagpond Vineyards, Sagaponack. 537-5106
Ternhaven Cellars, Greenport. 477-8737

ABOUT THE AUTHOR

Joan Reminick writes the Eats and Dining News & Notes columns for Newsday. She has worked as a journalist and has written both fiction and non-fiction for several national magazines; she also edits the Zagat Survey of Long Island Restaurants. In the past, Reminick has been a teacher of English and Humanities at both the college and high school levels. She received her master's degree from Hofstra University and her bachelor's from Brooklyn College. Born and raised in Brooklyn, she lives on Long Island with her husband and two children, now in college.

Editor
Phyllis Singer

Director of Editorial Design
Bob Eisner

Editorial Coordinator
Jeff Pijanowski

Marketing Manager
MeiPu Yang

Production Coordinator
Julian Stein